ISBN 978 1 905184 28 6

L M S JOURNAL

NUMBER EIGHTEEN

Contents

Gloucester, on the 'west road' from Birmingham, was well known to me during my time in the Little Bristol Link and the photographer, the late Eric Bruton, a good friend. This picture was taken on 9th May 1953 and shows the northbound 'Pines Express' headed by Class 5 No. 44851 departing from Eastgate station with a train of Stanier Period 3 stock painted in carmine and cream livery. Also visible is a British Railways Class 5MT No. 73014 at the head of an Ordinary Passenger Train whilst to the right an unidentified Class 3F appears to have been engaged on shunting duties.
ERIC BRUTON

Designed by Paul Karau
Printed by Amadeus Press, Cleckheaton
Published by WILD SWAN PUBLICATIONS LTD.
1-3 Hagbourne Road, Didcot, Oxon, OX11 8DP. Tel: 01235 816478

EDITORIAL

I hope readers will agree that we have an interesting mixture of articles for this edition of *LMS Journal*. One subject that has not been covered in any depth is the problems caused to the railways during the Second World War and the first of a series of separate articles recording these events appears in this edition. Graham Warburton's signal series examines the role of the Signal & Telegraph Department during the war whilst a short feature by Nelson Twells records the gift of three ambulances by the employees of some American railways to the LMS. Future editions will examine other aspects. Other articles in this issue cover a variety of subjects, including Peter Tatlow's major work on LMS breakdown cranes.

I was particularly pleased to receive the contribution from Barry Lane with the pictures that show the locomotive changeover on the inaugural 'Royal Scot' and Neil Burgess's carefully researched article on the Somerset & Dorset Joint line, while Jim Jackson's experiences of work on the London Tilbury & Southend section provided me with an insight into a rather different railway compared to my Saltley experiences. Finally, I should not overlook Keith Turton's article on Birmingham's coal traffic. Whilst the record of the various types of wagons that were privately rather than railway company owned is well covered, the record of the traffic they carried is rather sparse, so I am pleased to be able to cover this aspect of railway operation.

Turning to the second half of the year, I am delighted to be able to advise readers that this year's Warley Model Railway Exhibition, to be held at the NEC Birmingham on 1st and 2nd December, will be rather special. *LMS Journal/Midland Record* and the LMS Society have been invited to participate in an 'exhibition within an exhibition' that will record the 85th anniversary of the end of the pre-grouping era and the start of the grouping, and the 60th anniversary of the end of the grouping and the beginning of British Railways. In addition, there will be layouts depicting the post-1923 grouping and post-1948 British Railways eras.

Bob Essery
e-mail: bobessery@gowhite.com

Articles should be sent to LMS Journal, Wild Swan Publications Ltd., 1-3 Hagbourne Road, Didcot, Oxon, OX11 8DP. Please include SAE with all articles and illustrations submitted for return in case of non-acceptance. Authors must have permission to reproduce all photographs, drawings, etc, submitted.

The 'Royal Scot' coming to a stand on arrival at Carnforth on the main line just south of the station behind superheated 'Precursor' No. 5299 Vesuvius *and unnamed 'Claughton' No. 5934.*

The two LMS compounds Nos. 907 and 908 waiting next to the main line ready to take over the train and onward to Glasgow.

The two compounds being coupled on to the train of 15 coaches.

THE INAUGURAL 'ROYAL SCOT'

by BARRY C. LANE

THERE had long been a morning express to Scotland from Euston. The 10.0 am departure was however tied down to the agreement between the east and west coast companies after the 'Races to the North' of the nineteenth century, allowing a minimum journey time of eight and a quarter hours to Glasgow. In the latter years of the LNWR, the train was composed of through sections for both Glasgow and Edinburgh, each with its own restaurant car, and even a through portion for Aberdeen attached at the rear of the train. It was far from non-stop, however, and picked up passengers at Willesden Junction, Rugby and at Crewe, where it divided and from thence both sections ran non-stop to Carlisle.

It was 1927 when the 10.0 am departure from Euston took on a new importance. The old agreement between the east and west coast companies still applied but the management of the grouped railways competed by running the trains direct to Scotland for Edinburgh and Glasgow passengers only.

The east coast route under the LNER was flexing its muscles with the new A1 Pacifics designed by Gresley. The LMSR had nothing larger than the 'Claughton' 4–6–0s from the old LNWR and the newly-built Hughes 4–6–0s developed from the LYR design, and so double-heading was not unusual for the first few years following the grouping.

The 10.0 am departure from Euston was named the 'Royal Scot' on 11th July 1927 and ran without a booked stop to Scotland. It did, however, stop to change locomotives and crews at Carnforth. The locomotives on the first working were unnamed 'Claughton' No. 5934, with driver G. Stone and fireman A. Young in charge, and pilot locomotive 'Precursor' 4–4–0 No. 5299 *Vesuvius*, with driver T.H. Hudson and fireman J.W. Porter. The train amounted to 15 bogies, six for Edinburgh and nine for Glasgow, loading to 417 tons net and averaged 55mph for the 236 miles to Carnforth.

From Carnforth, the train proceeded north behind two of the new LMS compound 4–4–0s, Nos. 907 and 908 leaving five minutes ahead of schedule. Some spirited running followed. Shap summit was topped at 24 mph with both engines having full boiler pressure and blowing off slightly. The train was now eight minutes ahead of scheduled time and the next ten miles were covered at an average speed of 70 mph. At one point, it was reported to exceed 90 mph but at Southwaite, signal

With sanders working, the compounds are seen here starting the northbound train with Greyrigg and Shap banks ahead of the working.

All photographs COLLECTION BARRY C. LANE

The reverse working from Glasgow arriving at Carnforth behind compounds 904 and 901 with sixteen coaches weighing in at 455 tons, eight minutes ahead of schedule.

The southbound (up) working starting from Carnforth behind 'George V' class No. 5384 S. R. Graves and 'Claughton' No. 5956.

Cameronian heading the up 'Royal Scot' at Preston. As the noticeboard on the smokebox concealed the number plate and the tender was lettered 'LMS' rather than the customary engine number, the identity of the locomotive was a mystery for some time. The tender with the extra coal rails allowing higher coal capacity was paired with No. 6113 for working the non-stop train and this may have been one of the earliest such trips.

checks slowed the train to a crawl all the way through to Carlisle – but still ten minutes ahead of booked time.

Beattock was passed in a similar fashion to Shap and the train arrived at Symington at 5-04 pm, a full 13 minutes ahead of time. The Edinburgh portion was dropped there and the train of nine coaches for Glasgow carried on behind the two Polmadie compounds. Due to the somewhat unexpected arrival of the 'Royal Scot' so far ahead of time, the locomotive for the Edinburgh portion took some time to arrive and couple on. However, the ex-Caledonian 'Dunalastair' 4–4–0 No. 14350 built in 1904, easily managed to arrive at its final destination 18 minutes before time, according to the public timetable.

The situation continued until the new Royal Scot class took over the working in the summer of 1927. The LNER had taken to running non-stop to Newcastle. The LM&SR service therefore cut out the Carnforth stop, and ran the full 301 miles to Kingmore just north of Carlisle. The old agreement between the two compa-

nies still stood, so the way to compete was to make the 10.0 am departures from King's Cross and Euston run without stopping.

When the LNER advertised their world record schedule non-stop all the way to Edinburgh, 392¼ miles, in May 1928, the LM&SR stole their thunder by running the 'Royal Scot' on the previous Friday, 27th April, non-stop to Glasgow! This was accomplished by running the two sections of the 'Royal Scot' as separate trains to their final destinations of Glasgow and Edinburgh. Royal Scot class No. 6113 *Cameronian* was paired with one of three ex-Midland Railway tenders with high coal rails, to allow a greater coal capacity, allowing it to cover the 401.4 miles without refuelling. LMS compound No. 1054 managed the six-coach Edinburgh portion and at just under 400 miles claimed the British record for the longest non-stop run of a 4–4–0.

It was not until 1932 that the agreed 8¼ hour schedule was abandoned and, from then on, the 'Royal Scot' became a much

faster train even though the non-stop feature was relaxed. Of course the streamlined trains in the late 1930s eclipsed all these timings with their 6½ hour schedule ... but that is another story.

References
The Railway Magazine 1927
Titled Trains of Great Britain, Cecil J. Allen 1946
Passenger Trains Formations – LMS Region, Clive S. Carter 1987

LMS 36/50 TON STEAM BREAKDOWN CRANES
by PETER TATLOW

This picture illustrates Motherwell's 36 ton Cowans Sheldon crane before being strengthened in 1938/9. Note that the ends of the right-hand of each pair of propping girders had a large grab handle by which to withdraw them. Jacks and ratchet gear installed as part of the upgrading replaced these. The lining and LMS insignia can clearly be seen on the coal bunker, water tank and cab sides. For some unknown reason the left-hand propping girder was missing.
NATIONAL RAILWAY MUSEUM (DY 25250)

Another view on the same occasion. The vermilion ends with black border will be observed on the ends of the carriage. Note the large handles to the screw jacks on the relieving bogies.

NATIONAL RAILWAY MUSEUM (DY 25251)

This shows a breakdown crane at work when clearing a pile-up of goods wagons following the derailment of a train at an unknown location. Note the spreader beam attached to the ramshorn hook with a pair of brothers (chains) hanging down for lifting the bodies of carriages and wagons.

AUTHOR'S COLLECTION

AT the grouping in 1923, the LMS Railway inherited from its constituent companies 25 steam breakdown cranes of varying sizes, together with a number of small hand cranes that were allocated to the Motive Power Department for breakdown work. Many of the steam cranes were of only 15 ton maximum capacity and dated from the last decade of the previous century, but within the total there were five relatively modern 35/36 ton capacity cranes, together with two 25 ton and three 20 ton cranes that were not quite so up to date.[1&2] For example, the greatest capacity available on the Northern Division, short of borrowing the ex-North British 36 ton crane from St Margaret's, Edinburgh, or summoning a similar one from Preston, was 20 tons.

As the company's locomotive building programme got under way, the introduction of an increasing number of larger engines for use on the system as a whole meant that the small cranes were unable to cope, which meant that there was a need to bring in a larger crane from further afield. The larger classes of locomotive introduced are shown in *Table 1*.

During the early years of the grouping the LMS had an unenviable record of serious accidents and by 1930 these included: Diggle (5/7/23); Lytham (3/11/24); Leeds (8/9/26); Parkgate and Rawmarsh (19/11/26); Charfield (13/10/28); Dinwoodie (28/10/28); Ashchurch (8/1/29); and Doe Hill (12/1/29). It was becoming apparent, therefore, from these and the host of other more minor events,

that there was an urgent need for more high-capacity cranes to handle the larger engines in the event of their coming off the track due to derailment, or collision. Under the supervision of EH Lemon of the Outdoor Machinery Department, Derby, orders were placed in 1930 for six 36 ton cranes, but for some reason they were to be ordered from three different suppliers, and they are the subject of this article. The largest quantity, three, was provided by Cowans Sheldon & Co Ltd of Carlisle. These cranes could lift their maximum load to a radius of 25 feet. Two more cranes came from the works of Craven Bros (Manchester) and had a similar performance, being able to lift their maximum load at 24 foot radius. The last order was for a single crane from

During the Second World War, breakdown gangs were trained to carry out their work under conditions of gas attack. An early exercise, probably in 1942, was performed by an LMS crew, in front of an audience of officers from other companies, on the section of the Strathaven to Darvel line in the Southern Uplands of Scotland, which had been closed to all traffic on 11th September 1939. The Motherwell crane again, by now strengthened to 50 ton capacity and numbered RS1054/50, is seen lifting ex-Caledonian Railway 4—4—0 Dunalastair II class, LMS No. 14330. This locomotive was withdrawn in February 1941.

S. C. TOWNROE

Table 1 - LMS Locomotives over 60 Tons in Weight Supplied up to 31 December 1930

Date intr'd	Nos (At 31/12/30)	Wheel arrangement	Power classification	Class	No by 31 Dec 1930	Weight, excl. tender (T-C)
1/23	10434-10474	4-6-0	5P	Rebuilt Hughes 4 cyl	41	79-01
2/23	7930-7959	0-8-4T	7F	Crewe freight tank	30	88-00
5/23	2110-2134/51-60	4-4-2T	3P	Tilbury tank	35	71-10
'23	2270-3	0-6-2T	4F	NSR Tank	4	64-10
2/24	900-934, 1045-1199	4-4-0	4P	Compounds	190	61-14
3/24	11110-11119	4-6-4T	5P	Horwich Baltic tank	10	99-19
'24	5845	4-6-0	4P	Prince of Wales	1	66-05
11/25	14630-14649	4-6-0	4P	Caledonian 14630	2	74-15
7/25	9676-9680	2-8-0	7F	Somerset & Dorset	5	68-11
5/26	13000-13224	2-6-0	5P4F	Hughes/Fowler Crab	225	66-00
4/27	4967-4999	2-6-6-2T	-	Beyer-Garratt	33	148-15/152-10
7/27	6100-6169	4-6-0	6P	Royal Scot	70	84-18
'27	9646-9665	2-8-0	7F	ROD	20	73-17
12/27	2300-2374	2-6-4T	4P	Passenger tank	75	86-05
3/29	9500-9602	0-8-0	7F	Mineral	103	60-15
'29	6399	4-6-0	6P	High Pressure	1	87-2
3/30	15000-15020	2-6-2T	3P	Passenger tank	20	70-10
11/30	5971, 5902	4-6-0	5XP	Patriot	2	80-15
				Total	**867**	

Ransomes and Rapier of Ipswich, but in this case 36 tons could only be lifted to a radius of 20 feet. I have never been able to establish why the LMS spread its orders in this fashion, when one would have expected greater economy and consistency to have been obtained by having one supplier fulfil the entire order. Either it was a condition of purchases made possible by means of a Government loan at low rates of interest for the purpose of relieving unemployment in heavy industry, or perhaps delivery periods had something to do with it.

SUPPLY OF 36 TON CRANES

All six of these cranes were completed and delivered in 1931, being allocated in the first instance to Durran Hill (Carlisle), Leeds, Motherwell, Rugby, Newton Heath (Manchester) and Kentish Town (London), respectively. All had relieving bogies to spread the load while in train formation, one or both of which were capable of being detached at the site of operations to enable the crane to approach closer to the load to be lifted. This concept was originally patented by Sir (Fredrick) Wilfred Stokes KBE of Ransomes and Rapier in 1904 and consisted of a pair of bogies attached one at each end of, in this case, a four-axle crane carriage. Before moving off again in train formation, it was necessary to reinstate the bogies and, by a system of levers and jacks, to transfer a sig-

nificant proportion of the dead weight of the crane onto the bogies. All cranes had a minimum radius of 18 feet and maximum of 40 feet. Whilst by the time of their introduction two pairs of propping girders were generally considered satisfactory, the specification in this instance must have called for three pairs without screw jacks at the ends. As well as lifting (hoist), the cranes were required by steam propulsion to be able to carry out the motions of lifting the jib from an approximately horizontal position when resting in travelling condition on the match truck, to it working a radius of 40 to 18 feet (derrick); to rotate the whole superstructure and jib through 360 degrees (slew); and under its own power travel at slow speed at the site of operations.

In all three designs, the carriage consisted of two main longitudinal members with plate framing below carrying the axleguards, together with end plates to which the relieving bogies were attached. Below the longitudinal members were three pairs of transverse boxes containing the propping girders, while further transverse members in the same plain as the longitudinals supported the slewing ring. Within this steelwork was accommodated a train of gears, from a spindle through the king pin, to provide drive, if the clutches were engaged, to the two axles for the travelling motion. As well as the clutch wheels on the carriage side to engage the

travelling gear, hand wheels on each end of a common cross shaft applied the brake to all four wheels of the carriage.

On all the designs, the superstructure consisted of a cast steel base-plate sitting on the slewing ring and upon which was mounted a pair of vertical steel side plates, or crab sides. The jib foot rested on the front end, while the machinery was placed between them with a pair of cylinders on the outsides supplied by a boiler at the rear, with coal boxes and water feed tanks beside it and the counter weight behind or beneath. The boilers were Spencer Hopwood No. 14 squat hand coal fired with cold water feed, pressed to 120lb/sq in. The driver was positioned in front of the boiler and the derricking tackle attached to the crab side beside him. The whole superstructure could be rotated on the carriage by the slewing gear, while at the site of operations, clutches could be engaged to drive the forward two axles by the travelling gear.

COWANS SHELDON CRANES

The order for the Cowans Sheldon cranes was received on 30th May 1930 and was given Works Nos. 5111 to 5113.[3] They were the first built by the company to utilise the relieving bogie principle. In the Cowans design, the cantilever between the crane and bogie consists of a triangular system of tie and strut. The horizontal strut rested in a knuckle socket on the end

RS1054/50 was photographed in British Railways black livery at St. Margaret's on 30th May 1966. Note the additional tool and lumber boxes added to the relieving bogies and match wagon.

M. S. WELCH

This shows RS1001/50 while allocated to Springs Branch, Wigan, at work on bridgeworks at Rochdale on 20th August 1977, assisted by ex-LNER Ransomes & Rapier 45 ton crane No. RS1083/45 from Newton Heath. Note the propping girders drawn out and the jacks screwed down on timber packing, together with the diagonal hazard stripes on the water tanks, counterweight sides and propping girders.

M.S. WELCH

of the crane carriage. At the bogie end the strut and the inclined tie were connected and were supported by a lever and fulcrum on the bogie, which could be raised by a screw jack. As supplied, these cranes weighed 95 tons in working order with a maximum axle load of 13 tons, and 6 tons 16 cwt resting on the match wagon. The total weight of the crane and match wagon was therefore 111 tons 16 cwt. 3ft 1in diameter solid spoked wheels were provided on the crane and bogies with 12 by 6 inch diameter journals on the former, reduced to 9 by 5 inch journals on the latter.

The Cowans cranes had a double lattice jib formed of four longitudinal angles with diagonal bracing angles riveted inside to form a box section for the majority of its length, additional plates being used in the construction of the swan-neck jib head. The jib was raised by the derricking tackle consisting of ten parts of 4 inch circumference steel wire rope, one of which wound round the drum immediately in front of the driver's position. The double hook, or ramshorn, was hoisted by six parts of 3½-inch circumference steel wire rope, one being taken down to the hoisting drum close by the foot of the jib.

All four of these motions were driven by a pair of (in the case of the Cowans cranes) 12 inch by 8 inch diameter cylinders driving a cross shaft at the centre of the superstructure, acting on trains of bevel and spur gears brought into play by dog clutches for each motion. The final drive of the derricking motion was via a worm gear to aid control during lowering. The speed of hoisting could be increased for lighter loads by engaging a different set of gears. The steam was supplied by a 6ft 8in high 4ft 6in diameter boiler with a heating surface of 138.7 sq ft and 12.4 sq ft grate area which produced an evaporation rate of 1,055 lb/hr, or 1,400 lb/hr when worked hard. Thus the machinery enabled the jib to be raised from the match wagon to minimum radius in 3 minutes. 36 tons could be lifted at the rate of 13 feet per minute in low gear, or 12 tons at 35 feet per minute in high gear. One whole revolution of the superstructure with a 36 ton load took 2 minutes, while with a load of 10 tons the crane could propel itself along the track at 150 feet per minute.

One of the first tasks undertaken by one of the new Cowans Sheldon cranes must have been at Crich (Derbyshire), when in the first few moments of 17 June 1931 the

The jib-head of RS1054/50 resting on the match wagon No. M299855 at Haymarket on 30th June 1970. AUTHOR (35/98-32)

The jib-foot and live ring of RS1005/50 at Crewe Diesel Depot on 24th June 1972. Note the safe load indicator on the side of the jib and the casing enclosing the gear wheel to the hoisting drum. The cylinders were likewise encased on this crane, as part of a move towards increased safety. AUTHOR (35/108-10)

The rear three-quarters view of RS1005/50 at Crewe on the same day. Note the boiler safety valves, manholes, drain cocks and firebox dampers. AUTHOR (35/108-20)

The additional duty plate added to Cowans Sheldon cranes following strengthening in 1938, in this case No. RS1005/50. AUTHOR (35/108-16)

COWANS SHELDON & Co. Ltd CARLISLE
No 5636 LOADS NOT TO EXCEED 1938
50 TONS AT 18 FEET RADIUS PROPPED
45 TONS AT 20 FEET RADIUS PROPPED

double-headed Leeds to Bristol express ploughed into the rear of a mineral train near Ambergate.[4&5] Here one of the new Cowans Sheldon 36 ton cranes, presumably from Leeds, assisted by Derby's 36 ton Ransomes and Rapier of 1915 and an older 15 ton Cowans Sheldon crane, set about clearing up the wreckage and righting two overturned 4–4–0s and rerailing derailed coaches.

CRAVEN BROS CRANES

The Cravens cranes were given Order Nos. 12683–5 and were built by the company at their works in Reddish, Stockport. In the Cravens design of relieving bogie, the cantilever between the crane and bogie consists of a cast steel triangular frame, which slots into sockets within the crane carriage. At the bogie end, a scissors frame on the bogie, which can be raised

and lowered by a transverse threaded rod operated by a large hand wheel on one side, supports the cantilever. These cranes weighed 95 tons in working order with a maximum axle load of 12 tons 19 cwt. The total weight of the crane and match wagon was therefore 108 tons 2 cwt. 3ft 1in diameter ten solid-spoked wheels with 12 by 6½ diameter inch journals were provided on the crane, with the same sized

When new, one of the 36 ton Craven Bros cranes was allocated to the Motive Power Section at Rugby and later numbered RS1013/50. Here it is seen in 1936 with jib raised and attached to match wagon No. 299852. The left-hand relieving bogie had a wooden box added to carry timber packing. NATIONAL RAILWAY MUSEUM (DY25319)

wheels, but journals reduced to 9 by 5 inch on the bogies.

The crane had a double lattice jib formed of four longitudinal angles with transverse and diagonal bracing angles riveted outside to form a box section for the majority of its length, additional plates being used in the construction of the swan-neck jib head. Unlike the cranes supplied by the other two manufacturers,

A Craven crane positioned on a sharp curve to demonstrate the benefit of the articulated jib. Note that, despite the angle of the distant crane carriage to the nearer match wagon, the jib head was still central on the jib rest.
COLLECTION B. C. LANE

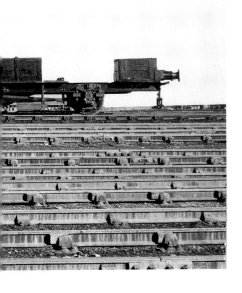

the Craven cranes had articulated jibs. This meant that, because the foot of the jib was slotted along the axis of the jib, when the crane and match truck were in travelling formation, as they entered a curve in the track, the head of the jib was free to move relative to the projected centre line of the crane and thereby maintain its approximate position on the match wagon. Otherwise it would have remained in line with the carriage of the crane, which would have caused the jib head to move to one side of the jib rest. When the jib was raised to the near vertical, however, the load was transferred to the crab sides through the crutch of the slot. The jib was raised by the derricking tackle consisting of two sets of six parts of 4-inch circumference steel wire rope, one from each set being wound round the drum immediately in front of the driver's position. As built, the double hook, or ramshorn, was hoisted by four parts of 4 inch circumference steel wire rope, two of which were taken down to the hoisting

drum close by the foot of the jib, the other two passing over a single block with a hook attached to the underside of the jib-head. All four motions were driven by a pair of 14 inch by 8 inch diameter cylinders driving a cross shaft, at a maximum velocity of 140 rpm, at the centre of the superstructure, acting on trains of bevel and spur gears brought into play by dog clutches for each motion. The steam was supplied by a 6ft 6in high, 4ft 6in diameter boiler with a heating surface of 150 sq ft and 12.5 sq ft grate area capable of producing an evaporation rate of 1,155 lb/hr, or 1,600 lb/hr when worked hard. The speed of hoisting could be increased for lighter loads by re-rigging the hoisting tackle. This somewhat time-consuming procedure was achieved by releasing the smaller block and hook from under the jib head and dispensing with the large ramshorn hook. The crane could propel itself at a speed of 6 mph.

One of the first tasks undertaken by one of the new Cravens cranes was in the cut-

13153 MUST HAVE BEEN SATISFACTORILY REPAIRED FOR IT WAS
NOT WITHDRAWN UNTIL 1963.
EDGE HILL 1933, BESCOT (AS 2853) 1948, NUNEATON 1960.

On 31st November 1931, LMS 2—6—0 No. 13153, which was built the previous year, was hauling a freight train when it ran into some empty coaching stock just north of Tring station. In this picture, the then nearly new Craven 36 ton breakdown crane, probably from Rugby, is seen at work during the clearing-up operation.

AUTHOR'S COLLECTION

This picture shows Rugby's crane when it was fitted with a jib extension to enable it to lift light loads to a greater height and is seen lifting an LMS 12 ton 5-plank open wagon high in the air. The ramshorn hook had been temporarily discarded and the smaller hook reeved over the jib extension.
NATIONAL RAILWAY MUSEUM (D15851)

No. RS1013/50 in early BR days wearing a black livery with little relief other than white jib head and counterweight, together with a red flywheel.

RS1013/50 at Carnforth on 22nd March 1981 in maroon livery shortly before withdrawal and sale to the East Lancashire Railway.

Soon after delivery, the Ransomes & Rapier 36 ton steam breakdown crane had arrived at the site of a freight train derailment on an unidentified length of quadruple track on Midland territory. Some wagons appear to have derailed on a trailing crossover, fouling both adjacent tracks and in effect blocking the whole line. Note the wagons placed on the ballast beyond the larger crane and another down the bank behind the signal.

AUTHOR'S COLLECTION

ting to the north of Tring station on 3rd November 1931, when a collision occurred between a freight train hauled by No. 13153 and No. 6791, which was hauling a train of empty coaching stock. This accident was soon followed by the smash at Great Bridgeford on 17th June 1932.[6–10] During the 1930s, the jib was temporarily lengthened to give a lift of 8 tons at 23 foot radius, but to a height of 54ft 6in above rail level for use on civil engineering applications, such as the reconstruction of engine shed roofs and at Birmingham New Street station. This alteration could be made in 50 minutes.

RANSOMES & RAPIER CRANE

The Ransomes & Rapier crane was built to Order No. D2958. Rapier were the pioneers, and original patentees, of the relieving bogie system and in their design the cantilever between the crane and bogie consisted of a riveted steel triangular frame, which slotted into sockets within the crane carriage. At the bogie end, the

cantilever was supported by a cross beam on the bogie, upon which a screw jack could be raised and lowered by a transverse threaded rod operated by a large hand wheel on top of the bogie. As supplied, this crane weighed 82 tons in working order with a maximum axle load of 12 tons 7 cwt. The total weight of the crane and match wagon was 107 tons 19 cwt. 3 ft 1in diameter wheels with 12 by 6½ diameter journals were provided on the crane, together with 3ft 5½in diameter disc wheels and journals reduced to 9 by 4½ inch diameter on the bogies.

The crane's jib was formed from a pair of vertical plates with flange angles and transverse and diagonal bracing angles riveted outside to form a box section for the majority of its length, additional transverse plates being used in the construction of the swan-neck jib head. The jib was raised by two sets of derricking tackle, each consisting of five parts of 4½ inch circumference steel wire rope, one from each being wound round the drum immediately in

front of the driver's position. The ramshorn was hoisted by four parts of 4¼ inch circumference steel wire rope, one of which was taken down to the hoisting drum behind the king post. The superstructure could be rotated on the carriage by the slewing gear, while at the site of operations, clutches could be engaged to drive the forward two axles by the travelling gear. All four of these motions were driven by a pair of 14 inch by 8 inch diameter cylinders driving a cross shaft at the centre of the superstructure acting on trains of bevel and spur gears brought into play by dog clutches for each motion. The final drive of the derricking motion was via a worm gear to aid control during lowering. The speed of hoisting could be increased for lighter loads by engaging a different set of gears.

This machinery could lift 36 tons at the rate of 10 feet per minute in low gear, or 10 tons at 40 feet per minute in high gear and enabled the jib to be derricked with loads at the rate of 6 feet per minute. One

After being transferred from Kentish Town to Holbeck in 1938, No. DE331159, formerly RS1004/40, stayed much of its life there until being withdrawn from Doncaster, from where it was sold to the Nene Valley Railway in December 1982. This photograph shows it at Holbeck on 10th June 1972 in bright red livery and paired with a former LNER match wagon.
AUTHOR (35/107-12)

A close-up view of DE331159 on the same occasion.
AUTHOR (107/14)

LMS match wagon No. 299852 as built at Derby in 1931. Note the small wheels permitting the lowered solebars to afford easier access for the crew to release and stow the ramshorn and other lifting equipment. This design of match wagon was paired with all six of the breakdown cranes supplied by Cowans Sheldon, Cravens Bros and Ransomes & Rapier to the LMS in 1931. NATIONAL RAILWAY MUSEUM (DY16924)

whole revolution of the superstructure with a 36 ton load took 1½ minutes, while with a load of 18 tons the crane could propel itself at 85 feet per minute.

Amongst the tasks undertaken by the Rapier crane were clearing up following an accident at Winwick Junction (16/10/39), when a double-headed express passenger train, No. 5544 leading, ploughed into the wreckage that was the result of a collision between a freight train and light engine.[11&12] It also attended at the accident at Grendon, between Atherstone and Polesworth (21/7/47), when an express passenger train hauled by No. 6244 derailed, due to defective track.[13-17]

MATCH WAGONS
The match wagons for all six cranes were designed and built by the LMS Railway Company at Derby Carriage & Wagon Works in 1931 to Lot 600, Nos. 299850 to 299855, tare 9 tons 3 cwt.[18] These wagons ran on 2ft 8½in diameter disc wheels with

9 by 4¼ inch journals. Conventional independent each-side brakes acting on both wheels were fitted and worked by right-handed levers. Match wagon No. 299850 paired with the Rapier crane No. RS1004/40 was replaced by wagon No. (DE)961652, formerly paired with a similar 35 ton Rapier crane supplied to the LNER in 1932. The latter was withdrawn in March 1970, after which the match wagon was presumably surplus and hence available for RS1004/40.

GENERAL
All the cranes could negotiate a minimum radius of 4 chains and were limited to a speed of 45 mph. The cranes, relieving bogies and match trucks were equipped with through pipe for the train vacuum brake, but were not fitted with vacuum brakes. The relieving bogies were not braked.

At first the cranes allocated to depots in England were given numbers in the MP

series, which was shown by a small cast plate attached to the carriage framework, but Scottish cranes received a plant number. In October 1941 the LMS introduced a new numbering scheme for all travelling rail-mounted and road cranes which commenced with an indication of the type of crane and concluded with its maximum capacity. The first letter was R or P, for rail-mounted or portable, while the second letter could be S for steam, D for diesel and M for manual powered machines. The middle four digits identified the particular crane. This renumbering postdated the strengthening of some of the cranes and all adopted the form RS10xx/50 or 40, as shown below, but these did not necessarily displace the previous numbers.

Details of the individual cranes and their allocation are given in the attached table.

Table 2 - Comparison of Crane Details

Item	Cowans Sheldon	Craven Bros	Ransomes & Rapier
Works or Order No.	5111 to 5113	12683-5	D2958
LMS Nos. (1941), RS10xx/50 or 40:	1001, 1005, 1054	1013, 1015	1004
Weight of crane in working order (T-c)	95-0	95-0	92-0
Max axle load (T-c)	13-0	12-19	12-7
Total weight with match truck (T-c)	111-16	108-2	107-19
Wheel diameter: crane/bogie (ft-in/No. of spokes or disc wheels)	3-1/10/3-1/10	3-1/10/3-1/10	3-1/10/3-5½/disc
Journal size: crane/bogie L x dia (in)	12 x 6/9 x 5	12 x 6½/9 x 5	12 x 6½/9 x 4½
Derricking rope (No. of parts/inch circum.)	10/4	2 x 6/4	2 x 5/4¼
Hoisting rope: as built - strengthened (parts/in circumference)	6/3½ - 6/4	2 x 2/4 – 2 x 3/4	4/4¼
Cylinders: stroke x dia (in)	12 x 8	14 x 8	14 x 9
Boiler: height x dia (ft-in)	6-8 x 4-6	6-6 x 4-6	U/k
Boiler pressure (lb/sq in)	120	120	120
Heating surface & grate area (sq ft)	138.7/12.4	150/12.5	u/k
Rate of evaporation: aver/max (lb/hour)	1,055/1,400	1,155/1,600	u/k
Speed of hoisting 36T/12 or 10 (ft/min)	13/35	u/k	10/40
Rotate 1 rev with 36T in (min)	2	u/k	1½
Speed of travel with 10 or 18T (ft/min)	150	528	85
Max radius to lift 36T (ft)	25	24	20

Note: u/k = Unknown.

Table 3 - LMS 36 Ton Steam Breakdown Cranes - Duties

Make		Cowans Sheldon		Cravens Bros		Ransomes & Rapier	
Load (Tons)		Propped	Free on Rail	Propped	Free on Rail	With outer/ inner props	Free on Rail
At radius (ft)							
As built	18	36	12	36	18	36/19	12
	20	36	12	36		36/19	12
	24	36	-	36	12	-	-
	25	36	8	-	-	-	-
	30	25	6	24	6	24/10½	6
	40	18	3½	18	3½	18/6½	3½
Strengthened	18	50	12	50	18	40/19	12

Table 4 - LMS Locomotives over 72 Tons in Weight Supplied between 1 January 1931 and 31 December 1938

Date intr'd	Nos	Wheel arrangement	Power classification	Class	No by 31 Dec 1938	Weight, excl. tender (T-C)
12/27	2375-2424	2-6-4T	4P	Passenger tank	50	86-05
11/30	5502-5551*	4-6-0	5XP	Patriot	50	80-15
7/33	6200-1/3-12	4-6-2	7P	Princess Royal	12	105-04
4/34	2500-2536	2-6-4T	4P	3 cylinder passenger tank	37	92-05
5/34	5552-5742	4-6-0	5XP	Silver Jubilee	191	79-11
8/34	5000-5471	4-6-0	5P5F	Black Five	452	72-12
6/35	8000-8097	2-8-0	7F	Freight	98	72-02
7/35	6202	4-6-2	7P	Turbomotive	1	110-11
10/35	6170	4-6-0	6P	Rebuilt Scot	1	84-01
12/35	2425-2494, 2537-2651	2-6-4T	4P	2 cylinder passenger tank	185	87-17
6/37	6220-6229	4-6-2	7P	Princess Coronation	10	108-02
6/37	6230-6234	4-6-2	7P	Duchess	5	105-05
				Total	**1,092**	

Notes: * Post 1934 numbers.

CAPACITY OF CRANES

The cranes' lifting performance at various radii when propped and therefore stationary, and 'free on rail' when it could travel under its own steam, are shown in *Table 3*. The loads quoted are for use on level track and super elevation had an adverse effect on these.

Table 1 lists various locomotive weights and this shows that some of them still exceed twice the new cranes' capacity, i.e. 72 tons assuming a crane at each end, by quite significant amounts in a few cases. The Garratts were clearly a case on their own, and one assumes that in the event of a derailment, the boiler would have to be separated from the frames to enable them to be handled as individual units. Nonetheless, this still left others, such as the large tank engines and the Royal Scots at nearly 85 tons. The weights quoted are for the engine in running order and therefore include water in the boiler and side tanks and coal in the firebox and bunkers of tank engines. My information is, however, that it was not usual to drain off the water or remove the coal before lifting. Whilst it may have been possible to empty the water tanks and bunkers of tank locomotives, it is quite likely that the boiler and firebox could not be drained if the locomotive was on its side.

It will be noticed that the Cowans and Craven cranes were designed to handle its maximum load of 36 tons from the minimum radius of 18 feet out to a maximum of respectively 25 and 24 feet. The stability of the crane is such that actually, as we shall see below, it can safely lift 50 tons at minimum radius. On the other hand, the Ransomes & Rapier crane could only lift its 36 ton load out to a radius of 20 feet. In addition, when lifting over the end, as opposed to over the side, even greater loads could be handled. In the less sophisticated days before the advent of Method Statements, the Health and Safety Executive and the like, the men in charge of breakdown work were left by management to get on with the work as they saw fit. They had the experience and the responsibility was theirs. For this reason, should a critical lift be undertaken, the careful supervisor would position a man at the rear of the crane to warn him as soon as any of the wheels of the crane started to lift off the rails. At accidents, after removing any dead and injured, and in the days before Police 'scene of crime' investigations, the priority was to clear the line and

restore traffic, and hence the railway's revenue, as soon as practical. In those days of loose-coupled hand-brake-only wagons, minor derailments, either out on the line, or more often in the marshalling or goods yard, were almost an everyday occurrence. The breakdown gangs became familiar with the tools of their trade, including the crane, if they had one, but equally the techniques of jacking and packing, hauling errant vehicles over rerailing ramps, etc could be employed. Of course, if the crane supervisor overdid it and tipped the crane over, he was likely to find himself without a job in economically difficult times. The number of incidents and cranes in use meant that occasionally the worst happened but, on the whole, a good job was done, with a lot of hard work involved, and the line reopened with the minimum of fuss.

STRENGTHENING OF COWANS AND CRAVEN CRANES TO 50 TONS CAPACITY

The LMS's locomotive building programme continued and, after the arrival of William Stanier in 1932, led to the introduction of even bigger engines, mainly in the form of his two classes of Pacifics. The 'declared' weights of further engines of over 72 tons built between 1st January 1931 and 31st December 1938 are shown in *Table 4*.

As with so much of the LMS Motive Power Department's activities during this period, it seems that a review of breakdown arrangements took place around 1937/8. As a result, instead of ordering new cranes of greater capacity to cope with the even bigger engines, the existing three Cowans Sheldon and two Craven Bros 36 ton cranes were strengthened and upgraded to a maximum capacity of 50 tons at their minimum radius of 18 feet. They were also concurrently fitted with screw jacks at the end of the propping girders. At the same time the above-mentioned single Ransomes and Rapier crane, together with its Midland Railway forerunner, for so long stationed at Derby, were uprated to 40 tons and jacks added to the ends of the propping girders of the former. The increase in capacity was really only in recognition of what the breakdown gangs were already doing anyway.

It was fortunate that the capacity of the five cranes was increased shortly before the outbreak of World War 2, when there were increasing demands made upon them

due to the effects of aerial bombardment and the requirements of the military authorities, which included mounting naval guns overlooking the Straits of Dover. It is perhaps for this reason that the LMS was able to forego the delivery of the 45 ton cranes that were supplied to the other three railways in 1939/40, as part of the Government's air-raid precautions, and at its expense, the LNER receiving six, GW four and SR two.[19&20] Instead later, even at the height of the war, the LMS was able to obtain sufficient priority, in competition with the other demands of war on industry, for the supply of eleven 30 ton cranes to undertake work beyond the abilities of old 15 ton cranes.[21&22]

In the case of the Cowans Sheldon 36 ton cranes, the order for the strengthening work to 50 ton capacity was placed on 28th August 1938 and carried out to Works Orders Nos. 6636 to 6638. In addition to the provision of jacks and ratchet gear to move the propping girders in and out, the main element of the work was the alteration of the hoisting rope from 3½ to 4in circumference, presumably requiring a new hoisting drum. This required the provision of new pulley wheels, but still of 2ft. 3in diameter and a larger ramshorn, while additional notice plates were fitted to indicate the increase in capacity. In its revised state the maximum height of lift to the ramshorn above rail level was 36ft 6in at minimum radius with a 34ft range, i.e. 2ft 6in above rail level.

By the time the order to strengthen their cranes was received, Craven Bros had been taken over by Herbert Morris at Loughborough, where the work was allocated to order No. C57/3478. Work on these cranes involved jacks and ratchet gear on the propping girders. Rather than increase the size of hoisting rope, however, the tackle was re-rigged to provide six instead of four parts. To achieve this the attachment of the small block carrying the return ropes to the underside of the jib was altered so that by adding two more pulley wheels at the jib head, the return ropes could be passed over them and return to the small block, now attached to the top of the new main block carrying the ramshorn.

Following strengthening, the three Cowans Sheldon and the two Craven cranes became the front line plant on the LMS for dealing with derailments, collisions and bridgeworks, and some adjustments to the allocations were made so that the 50 ton cranes were strategically positioned along the length of the West Coast main line at Willesden (London), Rugby, Crewe North, Kingmoor (Carlisle) and Motherwell, whilst the Rapier crane, now of nominal 40 ton capacity, went to Holbeck (Leeds). Therefore the 50 ton cranes were available to deal with Stanier's Pacifics should they become derailed and were the highest capacity cranes in mainline use in the country until the introduction of the 75 ton cranes in 1961 by British Railways. Up to nationalisation on 1st January 1948, the Cowans cranes are known to have assisted at accidents at Todmorden (4/9/42), Bourne End (30/9/45) and Polesworth (21/7/47), whilst one of the Craven cranes was used at Bourne End, when No. 6157 passed over a crossover at excessive speed and derailed.[23-27]

RUNAWAY CRANE AT GRISEBURN

On the evening of 28th November 1948 some wagons derailed in the loop at Griseburn Ballast Sidings between Crosby Garrett and Ormside on the former Midland Settle to Carlisle line, and as a result the goods brake van was thrown onto the Down line. The 50 ton Cowans Sheldon crane No. RS1001/50 from Kingmoor, Carlisle was summoned to clear the obstruction, arriving at 12.35 a.m. The line is on a 1 in 100 gradient at this point and arrangements were made to scotch the crane with a single wedged-shaped block of wood, once it was separated from the rest of the breakdown train. On completion of the work at about 2.30 a.m., the crane and its equipment were being packed away and it was time to bring the rest of the train closer prior to re-assembly. Despite the cautious efforts of Guard Cook, when the front portion met the match wagon, there was still enough energy to push the crane over the scotch block, after which the crane and match wagon started to run away down the hill.[28]

The foreman fitter George Campbell applied the hand brake of the match wagon on the cess side as soon as the crane started to move, ending up standing on the lever to gain greater purchase. Another fitter, Charles Campbell, was endeavouring to make his way along the crane on the same side towards the driver's position in order to lower the jib, while crane driver T S Baty was trying to do the same from the six-foot side. As if the runaway was not serious enough, 660 yards from the start of the crane's involuntary journey, the crane struck an overbridge.[29] At the time of the impact, the jib was almost lowered back on to the match wagon and was being held 2 feet above the jib rest, while the hook was stowed. Unfortunately, instead of lowering the jib the rest of the way, on hearing the warning shout, Baty jumped clear. At this moment the pulley wheels to the derricking tackle struck the soffit of the bridge. At least one pulley wheel fractured, allowing the jib to fall violently onto and fracture the jib rest. As a consequence, George Campbell was hit and fatally injured by flying debris. Charles Campbell and Baty were thrown off the crane and found at the lineside having sustained respectively a broken thigh and being dazed. Whilst no efforts had been made to sprag the wheels by inserting a bar or pole between the spokes of a wheel, Guard Cook had attempted to apply the hand brake wheel on the crane, but to no avail. Unable to read the labels in the dark, he failed to realise that, because it was one shaft continuous from one side to the other, its operation was handed and in fact he had been releasing the brake rather than apply-

ALLOCATION OF LMS 36/50 TON STEAM BREAKDOWN CRANES

LMS No MP No	5/41 No (2)	2nd BR No	Maker/ Works or Order No	Match wagon No	Remarks and Allocation	Wthn from BR	Disposal
MP2	RS1001/50	ADRC 95202	CS 5112/ 6637	299854	Durran Hill 2/31, Kingmoor by 2/36, to LMR '58, Lostock Hall *'62 to '69*, Springs Branch 2/72 to '79.	c '80	Sold 25/5/80 to MR Trust at Midland Rly Centre, Butterley
MP3	RS1004/40	ADRR 95207	R&R 2958	299850 961652	Kentish Town '31, Holbeck '38, to ER & No 159, later 331159, *6/72*, Doncaster ?.	c'79	Sold 12/82 to Nene Valley Rly, Wansford 1/83
MP4	RS1005/50	ADRC 95203	CS 5111/ 6636	299851	Leeds '31, Crewe N '39, Crewe S *11/65-6/72*, Springs Branch '79 to 8/80.	c'81	Sold to K&WVR 5/82
MP8	RS1013/50	ADRV 95205	Craven 12683/6	299852	Rugby '31, Crewe Wks (on loan) 6/45, Rugby 4/54, Derby '63, Cricklewood 12/68, Bescot 6/9/69, Longsight '73, Carlisle *'77 to '78*.	c'82	Sold to E Lancs Rly 8/82, Bury
MP9	RS1015/50	ADRV 95206	Craven 12683/6	299853	Newton Heath '31, Willesden c'39 to *7/58*, Derby c'62, Willesden 7/65 to 8/74+?, Allerton '81.	c'81	Sold to Dinting Rly Centre, KWVR, 30/9/90
1250 (Note 2)	RS1054/50	ADRC 95204	CS 5113/ 6638	299855	Motherwell '31, St Margaret's *'61 to 4/65*, Haymarket *'66 to '84*.	C'87	Sold to GWS at Didcot 9/87

Notes:
1. Dates shown in *italics* are spot dates upon which the crane is known to have been at the depot concerned.
2. The MP numbers series did not apply on the Northern Division in Scotland, which instead adopted a Plant No.
3. Makers: CS = Cowans Sheldon & Co Ltd, St Nicholas Works, Carlisle
   Craven = Craven Bros (Manchester) Ltd, Vauxhall Works, Reddish, Stockport
   R&R = Ransomes & Rapier Ltd, Waterside Works, Ipswich.

LIVERIES OF LMS 36/50 TON COWANS SHELDON STEAM BREAKDOWN CRANES

No / Item/Date	(RS1054/50) Pre 1939	RS1054/50 Post 1939	RS1001/50 Circa 1965	RS1001, 1005 & 1054/50 Circa 1970
Main body style	Lined crimson lake	Lined crimson lake	Lined maroon	Red
Lettering	Straw	Straw	Straw	White
Insignia	LMS coach insignia on coal bunker	LMS coach insignia on coal bunker & relieving bogie tool box	None	None or double ended arrow
Lining	Black and straw	Black and straw	Black and straw	None
Notice plates	Black on white		Black on white	White on red
Grab irons, steps and ladders	dark	dark	White	Black
Springs, hangers, axleboxes & carrying wheels	dark	dark	Black	Black
Brake wheels and levers	dark	dark	White	White
Buffer housings	Vermilion	dark	Red	Red
Buffer heads	Black	dark	Black	Black
CARRIAGE:				
Main side members	dark	dark	Lined maroon	Red
Underframes	dark	dark	Black	Black
Clutch wheels	dark	dark	Red	Yellow
Ends	Lined vermilion	Lined vermilion	Red	White and red or yellow stripes, or blk
Top		Black	Black	Black
Propping girders	dark	dark	Black	Black or y&bs
Rail clips	dark	dark	Black	Black
SUPERSTRUCTURE:				
Crab sides	Lined crimson	Lined crimson	Lined maroon	Red
Coal bunkers	Lined crimson	Lined crimson	Lined maroon	Red or y&bs to tank
Water tank sides	Lined crimson	Lined crimson	Y&bs	
Counter weight	Lined crimson	Lined crimson	Y&bs	Y&bs or red & white stripes
KEEP CLEAR notice	None	None	Red on white	None/Red on white
Boiler			Black	Black
Cylinder casing	Lined crimson	dark	Lined maroon	Red
Roof & canopy & platform and water tank tops	dark	dark	Black	Black
JIB AND TACKLE:				
Jib latticework	dark	dark	Maroon	Red
Jib head	Lined crimson	Lined crimson	Wh with bk letters & red doubling plt	Red/White
Bridle gear & pulley wheels	dark	dark	Black	Red
Lifting block and ram's-horn	dark	dark	Black	Orange
RELIEVING BOGIES:				
Main side members	Crimson lake	dark	Lined maroon	Red
Underframes	Black	dark	Black	Red or black
Inner ends	dark		Black	Black or red
Outer ends	Vermilion		Red	Red, black or y&bs
Load transmission yoke	dark		Black?	Black or red
Tool boxes	dark	Crimson lake	Black	Black
Tops	dark	dark	Black	Black
Lifting lugs on relieving bogies	dark	dark	Black	Yellow
MATCH WAGON:				
Body & tool boxes	Slate grey	dark	Black	Red, blk or r&wh stps
Lettering	White	White	White	White
Solebar, headstocks & buffer shanks	Slate grey	dark	Black	Black
Insides and floor	dark	dark	Black	Black
Jib support	Slate grey	dark	Black	Black

LIVERIES OF LMS 36/50 TON CRAVEN & 36/40 RAPIER STEAM BREAKDOWN CRANES

No Item/Date	RS1013/50 Pre-1939	RS1013/50 1960	RS1013 & 1015/50 1969-73	RS1004/40 1972
Main body style without lining	Black	Black	Crimson lake	Red
Lettering	White or straw	White	White	White
Insignia	None	None	Double arrow	None
Notice plates	Light on dark	White on red	White on red	Black on white
Grab irons, steps and ladders	Black	Black	White	
Springs, hangers, axleboxes & carrying wheels	Black	Black	Black	Red
Brake wheels and levers	Black	White	White	White
Buffer housings	Black	Red	Crimson lake	Red
Buffer heads	Black	Black	Black	Black
CARRIAGE:				
Main side members	Black	Black	Crimson lake	Red
Underframes	Black	Black	Black	Red
Clutch wheels	Black	White		White
Ends	Black	Black	Black	Red
Top		Black		
Propping girders	Black	Black	Yellow	Red white jacks
Rail clips	Black	Black	Yellow	
SUPERSTRUCTURE:				
Crab sides	Black	Black	Crimson lake	Red
Coal bunkers	Black	Black	Crimson lake	Yellow & blk stripes
Water tank sides	Black	Black	Yellow & blk stripes	Yellow & blk stripes
Counter weight	Black	Bk later white	Yellow & blk stripes	Yellow & blk stripes
KEEP CLEAR notice	None	None	Red on white	Red on white
Boiler	Black	Black	Black	Enclosed, y&bs
Cylinder casing	Black	Black	Crimson lake	Red
Roof & canopy & platform and water tank tops	Black	Black	Black	Black
Flywheel	Black	Red	Crimson lake	Red with white rim
JIB AND TACKLE:				
Jib lattice/plate work	Black	Black	Crimson lake	Red
Jib head	Black	White	White	White
Maker's plate	Light on dark	White on red	White or yellow on red	None
Bridle gear & pulley wheels	Black	Black	Black	Red
Lifting block and ram's-horn	Black	Black	Orange	Orange/black
RELIEVING BOGIES:				
Main side members	Black	Black	Crimson lake	Red
Underframes	Black	Black	Black	Red
Inner ends	Black	Black	Black	Red
Outer ends	Black	Red	Red	Red
Hand wheel	Black	Light		
Tool boxes	Black	Black	Black	None
MATCH WAGON:				
Body & tool boxes	Slate grey	Black	Crimson lake	Red
Lettering	White	White	White	White
Solebar, headstocks and buffer shanks	Slate grey	Black	Black	Red
Jib support	Slate grey	Black	Black	Red

Key:

Blk	=	Black	r&wh stps	=	Red and white stripes
Y&bs	=	Yellow and black stripes	N/A	=	Not applicable

Dark – see explanation on page 27

ing it! In any case, it required three complete turns to apply the brake fully.

The line North from Ais Gill summit generally falls all the way to Carlisle, 36 miles away from the scene of the accident. Fortunately, a short adverse incline beyond Lazonby was sufficient to bring the crane to a halt. Even so, it had already run nearly 23 miles, before gently rolling back into the station where, once at rest, the somewhat relieved signalman secured it. Nonetheless, prior to this, Control felt it necessary to make arrangements to clear the line through Carlisle station. Intercepting the runaway crane by loco-motive was even considered, but in the event such drastic action was not required.

LIVERIES

Without the benefit of a written paint specification and before the days of colour photography, it is very difficult to be pre-cise about the livery carried by LMS cranes. Monochrome photographs suggest that some at least were likely to have been black, but equally it is clear that No. RS1054/50, together with other break-down cranes on the Northern Division, had the crimson lake lined locomotive livery applied with coach insignia. Yet the match wagons may have remained in the goods wagon livery, although possibly in slate, rather than light to mid grey. In the case of the Motherwell crane, this style is evident both before and after strengthen-ing. There is, however, no evidence that I have come across to confirm whether this crane wore this from new (indeed, there is a hint that initially it may also have been black) or that the other cranes considered here ever carried a red livery during the LMS period.[30] In the table below, there-fore, regretfully an indication of 'dark', means that I am unable to be certain that an item was painted in crimson lake, black or some other non-reflective colour.

By the 1950s when owned by British Railways, all six cranes seem to have been out-shopped in a black, but in July 1959 a general instruction was issued that, as breakdown cranes went through the workshops for overhaul, they were to be repainted bright red.[31] Although the new 30 and 75 ton cranes delivered by Cowans Sheldon during the next few years were fully lined in straw and black, this does not generally seem to have been applied to existing cranes. No. RS1001/50, however, by the late sixties was painted in maroon with black and straw lining to the coal

bunker and solebars of the crane and relieving bogies,[32] whilst in 1964 No. RS1013/50 was out-shopped with a lined panel containing the 'ferret and dart board' insignia on the water tank.

Amazingly, upon withdrawal from BR, all six cranes have passed into the hands of private owners and will be found on pre-served railway lines. When it was with-drawn from Haymarket in 1987, RS1054/50 was the last steam breakdown crane in use on BR, after which it was acquired by the Great Western Society at Didcot.

ACKNOWLEDGEMENTS

No project of this nature is undertaken without the assistance of a great many people over the years and some contacts were so long ago, that I may have over-looked one or two. Initial help came from the Public Relations & Publicity Officer of the London Midland Region at Euston. Access was granted to the archives by the CMEs of both the London Midland and Scottish regions at Derby and Glasgow respectively. Permits to visit motive power depots were issued to myself and others, thereby enabling photographs to be taken of these and other cranes. Facilities were also afforded by Cowans Sheldon, Herbert Morris, Ransomes and Rapier and the Cumbria County Records Office. Correspondence has been entered into with various fellow enthusiasts and rail-waymen, of which perhaps the late Jack Templeton, Duncan Burton (a member of the LMS Society until his untimely death) and WM Roscoe Taylor deserve special mention. My thanks to them all, thus enabling me to offer this article.

REFERENCES:

1. Tatlow P, 'LMS breakdown arrangements', *British Railway Journal, LMS Special Issue*, (1988), pp43–48.
2. Tatlow P, 'Railway/Steam cranes – Cowans Sheldon 15 ton steam breakdown cranes', Parts 1 to 4, *Model Railways*, March, April, August, December 1990, p136–140, 206–210, 426–429 & 637–640.
3. Tatlow P, 'LMS Cowans Sheldon steam break-down cranes', *British Railway Modelling*, April 2004, p50–53.
4. Earnshaw A, *Trains in trouble No 6*, Atlantic Transport Publishers, 1990.
5. Earnshaw A, *An illustrated history of trains in trou-ble*, Atlantic Transport Publishers, 1996.
6. Hoole K, *Trains in Trouble, Vol 3*, Atlantic Transport Publishers, 1982, p29.
7. Whitehouse PB & St John Thomas D, *LMS 150*, David & Charles, 1987, p94.
8. Twells HN, *LMS miscellany*, OPC, 1982, pl.131.
9. Hamilton Ellis CH, *London Midland & Scottish, a railway in retrospect*, Ian Allan, 1970, p120.
10. Hall S, *ABC of railway accidents*, Ian Allan, 1997, p30.
11. Earnshaw A, *Trains in Trouble, Vol 6*, Atlantic, 1990, p22.
12. Earnshaw A & Jenkinson D, *The last years of the big four*, Atlantic, 1997, p98.
13. Earnshaw A, *Trains in Trouble, Vol 5*, Atlantic, 1980–93, p31.
14. Twells HN, *LMS miscellany*, OPC, 1982, pl.134–7.
15. Hamilton Ellis CH, *London Midland & Scottish, a railway in retrospect*, Ian Allan, 1970, p202.
16. Allen CJ, *The Stanier Pacifics of the LMS*, Ian Allan, 1950, p50.
17. Hall S, *ABC of railway accidents*, Ian Allan, 1997, pp24–25.
18. Essery RJ, *An illustrated history of LMS wagons, Vol 1*, Oxford Publishing Co, 1981, p152.
19. Tatlow P, 'LNER Cowans Sheldon 35/6 and 45-ton steam breakdown cranes', *Backtrack Special Issue No 2, The London & North Eastern Railway*, 2001, pp66–71.
20. Tatlow P, 'Ransomes & Rapier 45 ton steam breakdown crane', *British Railway Modelling*, Sept 2001, pp54–57.
21. Tatlow P, 'LMS 30 ton Cowans Sheldon steam breakdown crane', *Model Railways*. October 1972, pp797–804.
22. Tatlow P, 'Ransomes & Rapier 30 ton steam breakdown crane', *Railway Modeller*, November 1971, pp367–369 and January 1972, p24.
23. Hamilton JAB, *Rails to Nowhere*, G Allen & Unwin, 1981, pp62–5.
24. Trevena A, *Trains in Trouble, Vol 2*, Atlantic, 1981, p32.
25. Hamilton Ellis CH, *London Midland & Scottish, a railway in retrospect*, Ian Allan, 1970, p189.
26. Nock OS, *A history of the LMS, Vol 3*, George Allen & Unwin, 1983, pp71–73.
27. Hall S, *ABC of railway accidents*, Ian Allan, 1997, pp16–18.
28. Accident report, Ministry of Transport, 1949.
29. *The Railway Gazette*, 17 June 1949, p678.
30. Brownlie JS, *Railway steam cranes*, author, 1973, fig. 48.
31. British Railways, *General Instructions 10 – Covering the treatment of … breakdown cranes and other service stock*, July 1959.
32. Ashcroft W, 'Derailed at Hest Bank', *Steam World*, August 1998, pp58–61.

London & North Western Railway.
Chief Mechanical Engineers Office.
Crewe

Reference to your Letter.

TELEGRAMS–COOKE, CREWE. ALL LETTERS ON BUSINESS TO BE FULLY ADDRESSED C.J.B. COOKE, L. & N.W. RAILWAY, CREWE. TELEPHONE–120, CREWE.

In your reply give this reference. L.

February 8th 1913.

Dear Sir Gilbert,

There were a lot of newspaper people taking snap shots of the new engine the other day at Stockport and Manchester, and I enclose a couple of newspapers giving reproductions of photographs of the engine. You will see that in accordance with your wishes I have been running the engine about incognito. So far, we have every reason to be satisfied with its performance, but tomorrow I am hoping to give it a run to Rugby and back with a big load behind it, after which I propose to put the nameplate on and put the engine on ordinary working.

Yours faithfully,

C. J. B. Cooke

Enclo:

Sir Gilbert Claughton, Bart.,
The Priory,
DUDLEY,
Worc.

C.J. BOWEN COOKE.
Chief Mechanical Engineer.

TELEGRAMS–BOWEN COOKE, CREWE.
~~Postal Telegrams, COOKE, CREWE.~~
Telephone–120 CREWE.

London & North Western Railway.
Chief Mechanical Engineers Office.
Crewe

Reference to your Letter.

In your reply give this reference. L/DO.

October 7th, 1913.

Dear Sir Gilbert,

Referring to our conversation. I have pleasure in sending you herewith a comparative statement of the leading particulars of the L. & N. W. Engine "Sir Gilbert Claughton" and the Great Central Engine, "Sir Sam Fay" for your information.

Enclos.

Yours faithfully,

C. J. B. Cooke

Sir Gilbert Claughton, Bart.,
The Priory,
Dudley,
WORCESTERSHIRE.

FURTHER INFORMATION ON
THE CLAUGHTONS

Notes by BOB ESSERY

This undated broadside view of ex-L&NWR No. 2204 Sir Herbert Walker, *which became LMS No. 5926, was taken after 1923. Note the LMS emblem on the cabside of the Compound at the far right of the picture. The L&NWR cabside number plate had been removed so it is probable that this picture was taken when the locomotive received its LMS stock number, which, according to Baxter,* British Locomotive Catalogue 1825-1923 *Volume 2B, was June 1926.*
G. W. SHOTT

On more than one occasion I have found that after investigating every source and being reasonably certain that no further information is likely to emerge, you go to print and then within a very short time new material comes to light. Fortunately, with *LMS Journal*, we have, as contributor Phil Chopping has remarked a few times, a vehicle to absorb the fresh information. The LMS Society have undertaken to provide a comprehensive index for *LMS Journal*, so perhaps I should get to the point of this introductory note.

No. 3 of *Historical Locomotive Monographs, The Claughton & Patriot 4—6—0s* was published in December 2006 and launched at the Warley NEC Exhibition. During the two days of the show we met many readers and one, Mr. Pritchett, expressed interest in the new book and said that he had some papers that might be of interest. A few days later they arrived and since they added to what had been written, I felt that they should be published along with some of the pictures that we did not include in the volume. I would like to publicly thank Mr. Pritchett for his kindness and to say that I never cease to be grateful for the

generosity shown by readers who supply pieces of information that we are able to share with readers.

THE LETTERS
On page 9 of the Monograph we refer to the trial run to Rugby with a train of 400-420 tons and the first letter reproduced here refers to the forthcoming event. It is also interesting for a number of points. First, why did Sir Gilbert wish the engine to run incognito? Furthermore, the letter is addressed to Sir Gilbert's home address and not to his office at Euston. The final point is that modern writers, the authors included, refer to the Chief Mechanical Engineer as Bowen Cooke, but on the letterhead the name is C. J. B. Cooke.

A few months later in October it is clear that Sir Gilbert wanted to know how the Claughton class compared to the Great Central 'Sir Sam Fay' class of 4—6—0s and his letter included a schedule that had been prepared by the Crewe Works Drawing Office.

Continued on page 33

GEO. HUGHES,
CHIEF MECHANICAL
AND
ELECTRICAL ENGINEER.

TELEPHONE: HORWICH 34.
TELEGRAMS: LOCO. HORWICH

LONDON AND NORTH WESTERN RAILWAY COMPANY.

P.

CHIEF MECHANICAL AND ELECTRICAL ENGINEER'S OFFICE.

HORWICH (S.O.), LANCS.,
Friday, 16th March 1923.

u/
Do/
REFERENCE.

R. C. Irwin, Esq.,
Euston Station,
LONDON. LNW. 1.

Dear Sir,

PERFORMANCE OF L.M.S.R. LOCOMOTIVES.

With reference to your letter of the 8th March 1923,
enclosing communication from Mr. J.C. Crebbin, addressed to
the Chairman. Briefly, the figures given by Mr. Crebbin for
the "Claughton" engines are:-

70 to 75 lbs. coal per train mile

and for the Paris, Lyons and Mediterranean Rly. 4-6-2 Locomotives:-

40 lbs. coal per train mile.

All the information at my disposal goes to show that
the figures in both cases are incorrect. Tests made on the
Paris, Lyons and Mediterranean Rly. in 1913, show

67 to 77 lbs. coal per train mile, or
.245 to .121 lbs per ton mile

with loads 273 to 635 tons respectively.

Quite recently we had our "Claughton" engines under
observation in actual service, and the results show a comparison
of

56 lbs. per train mile, or
.1946 lbs. per ton mile

(continued)

GEO HUGHES,
CHIEF MECHANICAL
AND
ELECTRICAL ENGINEER.

TELEPHONE: HORWICH 34.
TELEGRAMS: NORTHWESTERN, HORWICH

LONDON AND NORTH WESTERN RAILWAY COMPANY.

P.

CHIEF MECHANICAL AND ELECTRICAL ENGINEER'S OFFICE.

HORWICH (S.O.), LANCS.,
Friday, 16th March 1923.

u/
Do/
REFERENCE.

R. C. Irwin, Esq., LONDON.

PERFORMANCE OF L.M.S.R. LOCOMOTIVES. .... 2.

with an average load of 285 tons, including Shap incline.

From these figures you will see that Mr. Crebbin's
remarks are quite valueless. Of course, there are many
factors affecting coal consumption in "Locomotive Performance,"
of which the layman has no idea, and I do not think I need
bother you with a statement of them.

As regards the smokebox ash ejector, I can only say
that on long non-stop heavy trains this is practically indis-
pensible, and I am contemplating fitting a similar arrangement
to the large Horwich engines which are now working between
Crewe and Carlisle. I am not aware that this causes any
real discomfort to the passengers.

Yours truly,

Geo. Hughes

Taken at Camden on 6th May 1933, this photograph typifies the Claughton Class in their post-1928 LMS red livery. No. 5915 Robert Guiness was built in September 1914 and renumbered by the LMS in June 1927; the locomotive was withdrawn from service in November 1934. Note that the cab had been altered to the profile required to enable the engine to run on the Midland Division of the LMS. COLLECTION R. J. ESSERY

Old L&NWR No. 42 Princess Louise, *which became LMS No. 6004 in October 1926, was built in August 1920 and rebuilt with a large boiler in April 1928; the name was removed in June 1935. Although allotted a British Railways number, it was not applied and the locomotive, as the final member of the class, was withdrawn in April 1949. This rather impressive picture shows No. 6004 on an express passenger train, but, unfortunately, I have not been able to identify the location.* COLLECTION R. J. ESSERY

CHIEF MECHANICAL ENGINEER'S OFFICE,

DERBY.

2nd October, 1929.

TO THE LOCOMOTIVE AND ELECTRICAL COMMITTEE.

Gentlemen,

"CLAUGHTON" LOCOMOTIVES.

There are 129 "Claughton" engines which were built between 1913 and 1919, for the purpose of working heavy passenger trains on the old London & North Western system. They have not given the satisfaction that was hoped for, being very heavy in coal and water consumption and also in shed maintenance. During 1927 and 1928, 20 of these engines were fitted with an improved design of boiler, these engines being known as 5X Class. The steaming of these 20 engines is reported as satisfactory, but the engines are still not as efficient as they should be, and it is considered that there is still considerable room for improvement on the existing design of the cylinders and motion arrangement. In addition to the foregoing, there are several other details which it is proposed should be improved.

The question of the cylinder design has been thoroughly gone into, and it is proposed to rebuild two of the "Claughton" engines as three cylinder engines, with an independent valve gear to each cylinder, on similar lines to the "Royal Scot" engines. The improved type of boiler as used on the 5X Class "Claughton" engines would also be provided, and for these two engines standard 3,500 gallon tenders would be temporarily found for them.

The estimated cost of the alterations per engine would be £1,850, or £3,700 for the two engines, plus £600, cost of certain patterns, making a total estimated cost for the work of £4,300.

It will be remembered that 10 of the 5X Class "Claughton" engines have been fitted with the Caprotti valve gear, which, although giving an improvement in coal consumption, has, possibly owing to the newness of design, given trouble in some details, and has so far been expensive in shed repairs, although it is hoped that these difficulties may be overcome.

I shall be glad to have the Directors' sanction for the rebuilding of two "Claughton" engines with three cylinders as described above, to enable me to put this work in hand early, so that running tests may be carried out during the heavy summer traffic next year. These tests would then enable a decision to be made with regard to the remainder of this class of engine.

The submission of the proposal is approved by the Executive Committee and the allocation of the cost will be reported subsequently.

Yours faithfully,

HY. FOWLER.

There are not many pictures of Claughtons working on the Midland Division but I am able to include this picture of the pioneer engine, No. 5900 Sir Gilbert Claughton, at the head of the down Thames Clyde express at Leicester on 4th August 1934. What I have never found is any reference to what the old Midland Railway enginemen thought of the 'foreigners', as locomotives from another railway would have been described. What can be said is that the Class 5P Claughton would have been allowed to haul a heavier train than the Class 4P Compound.   H. N. JAMES

It is clear from the correspondence between R. C. Irwin and the LMS Chief Mechanical Engineer that Mr. Crebin was asking the LMS Chairman some 'interesting' questions; perhaps he was a major shareholder and was keen to ensure that the company was efficient in order to maintain the dividends paid to shareholders. However, as a result, we are able to publish a rather interesting letter. At this time locomotive performance was a topic that commanded considerable interest from certain sections of the public as reference to the contemporary magazines will confirm.

The final letter is dated 2nd October 1929 and was addressed to the Locomotive and Electrical Committee. At first sight it is a simple statement from the CME to the committee about the condition of the Claughton class locomotives at that date, but in my view there is rather more to it. Many authors have suggested that the CME was 'all powerful' and set the direction the company's locomotive policy would follow. This is particularly true when reference is made to Sir William Stanier, who, less than three years after this letter was written, was to be CME of the LMS. If anything, this letter confirms that policy began with a recommendation from the CME to the appropriate committee (the LMS changed the name of this committee more than once during the Company's lifetime) and if the committee approved, it went to the Board of Directors who usually accepted the recommendation. It is also worth noting that costs were carefully controlled and the money spent was allocated accordingly.

The final picture shows a Claughton shortly after it had been rebuilt as a Patriot. Taken on 7th August 1932, this photograph shows old L&NWR No. 2426, which was built in October 1917, and became LMS No. 5959 in October 1926. The locomotive was rebuilt as a Patriot in July 1932, and named Royal Naval Division *on 5th June 1937. When photographed, it was at the head of the down 'Welshman' express passenger train near Rugeley.*

W. L. GOOD

LMS SIGNALS
NO. 16 LMS SIGNAL AND TELEGRAPH STAFF IN WORLD WAR II
by L. G. WARBURTON

TABLE 1 – LMS Signal & Telegraph Department staffing 1938 to 1943.

| Year | WAGES STAFF | | | | SALARIED STAFF | | | | | Total Female Staff | Total Wages Staff F. included. | Total Salaried Staff F. included, | Grand Total |
| | Conciliation | | Artizan | | Clerical | | Technical | | Super-visory | | | | |
	Male	Female	Male	Female	Male	Female	Male	Female					
1938	3,058	11	947	11	132	53	160	14	125	89	4,027	484	4,511
1939	2,969	11	906	12	120	55	146	15	133	93	3,898	469	4,367
1940	3,034	11	912	12	118	57	152	16	128	96	3,969	471	4,440
1941	2,988	12	871	33	103	65	147	17	127	127	3,904	459	4,363
1942	2,952	41	852	38	94	64	145	17	129	160	3,883	449	4,332
1943	2,927	38	818	52	91	64	139	17	127	171	3,835	438	4,273

*L*MS *Journal* 15 dealt with the organisation of the S&T Department, which is concluded here with recognition of the tremendous effort made by the staff during World War II with the preparation and construction of war schemes, repair of bomb damage and so on. Staff members were also called up or volunteered for service in the war.

This article covers the time up to March 1944 from a staffing viewpoint as A. F. Bound retired in that year, although by this time there was little doubt as to the outcome of the war, but nevertheless there are sure to be a few more casualties and possibly honours and commissions not included here. The article was, in part, prepared from a report written by A.F.Bound, the Signal & Telegraph Engineer, covering the period 1939 to 1944.

Table 1 shows the total staffing of the department from which it can be seen that the number employed dropped by 238 between 1938 and 1943 and unsurprisingly, the number of women employed increased by 90. Wages staff were reduced by 192 and salaried staff by 46.

At the outbreak of the war, 244 men joined the armed forces, 175 were Reservists or Territorials, the remainder volunteers. 42% were from the labouring grades which at that time could be replaced, but the biggest problem lay with the loss of 11 skilled instrument makers from the Crewe, Gresty Road Telegraph Shops, where for more than two years overtime had been worked to keep pace with demand.

Linemen and their assistants were also a serious loss, with 49 leaving the department. The Government schedule of reserved occupations fortunately allowed the majority of staff to be retained and thereafter most losses during the war years were confined to retirement, ill health or to other industry, also men were allowed to remain at work after reaching the retirement age of 65.

Up to and including March 1944 the number of serving staff was:

Salaried Staff (England & Wales)	47 or 12%.
Wages Staff ditto	291 or 9%.
Salaried Staff (Scotland)	5 or 6%.
Wages Staff ditto	59 or 9%.

Casualties:
5 men missing and believed killed.
1 man accidently drowned.
1 man accidently killed.
11 men Prisoners of War.
3 men discharged due to War Injuries.

Commissioned Staff
Navy – 2 Lieutenants.
Army – 2 Lieut. Colonels; 3 Majors (1 discharged); 1 Captain & 6 Lieutenants.
Air Force – 1 Flying Officer and 1 Pilot Officer who was killed in action.

Decorations
C. Nelson, an Installer at Willesden – DCM.
H. J. A. Dyer, a Fitter at Barking – DFM.
G. Morris, an Inspector at Preston – mentioned in *London Gazette*, December 1940. Distinguished service France & Flanders.
V. Mitchell, an Area Technical Assistant at Bolton ditto.
D. S. Jewell, a Technical Assistant at Headquarters – mentioned in *The London Gazette*.
S. Hollinshead, a Labourer at Tyldesley – Received an official letter in connection with his remarkable courage in his first action at sea with the 2nd Maritime Battery when one aircraft appeared to have fallen to Hollinshead's gun individually.
T. Brown, a Messenger at the Divisional Office, Glasgow – Mentioned in despatches in respect of Personal Occurrence – extinguishing fire in RAF Armoury.

Civil Awards
J. H. Mottram, the Area technical Assistant at Rugby – MBE.
A. Wilson, a Lineman at Poplar – Mentioned in Supplement to *London Gazette*.
J. J. Freshwater, a Ganger at Barking – BEM.

Fig. 1. LMS Drawing 43037 detailing the LMS ARP signal box.

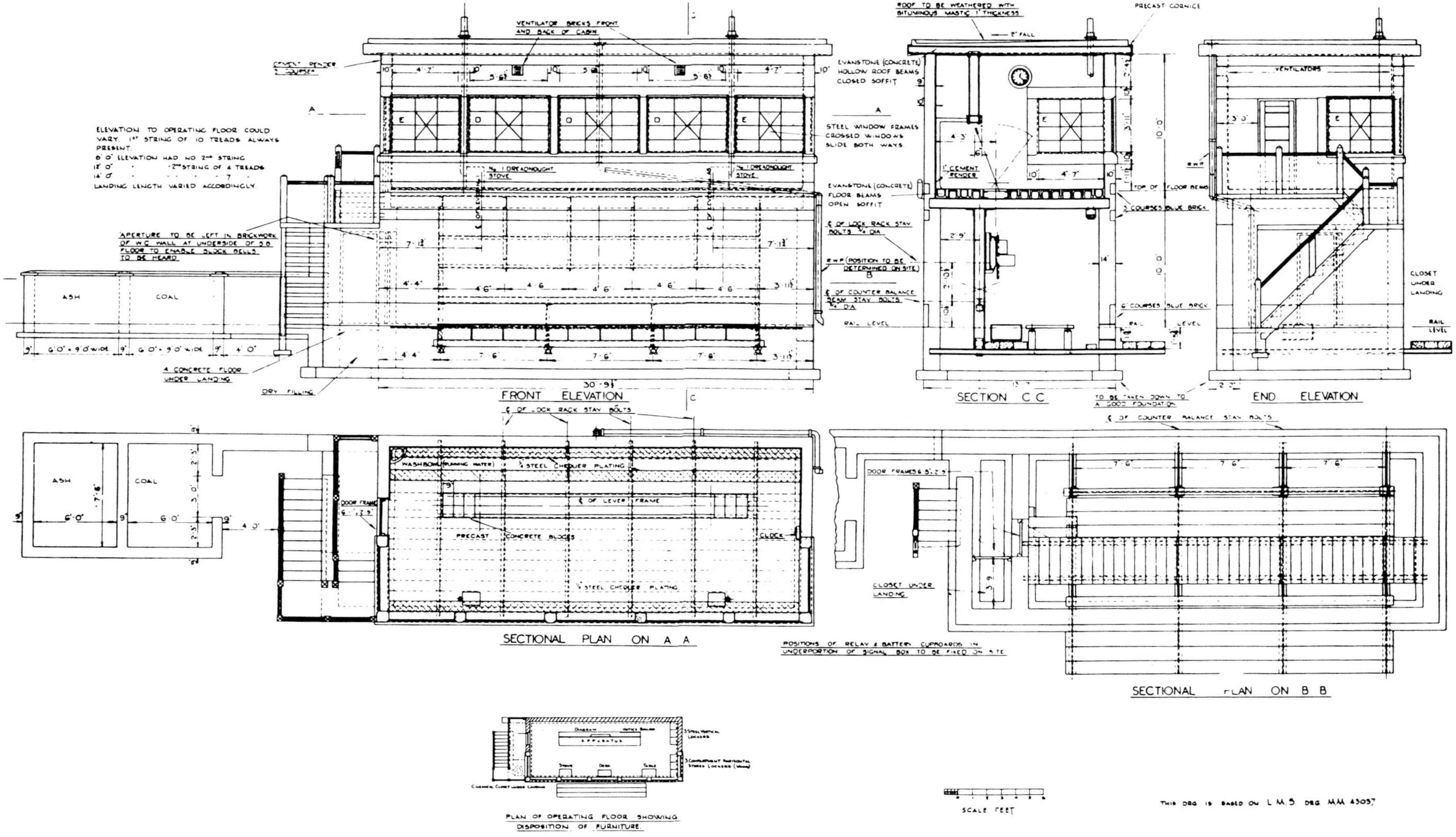

Plate 1. *Carlisle No. 12 signal box of ARP design. Apart from the basement windows and a steel staircase, the construction is as the drawing.*
PETER ROBINSON

As far as the LMS as a whole is concerned, according to G. C. Nash, in the book *LMS at War*, the LMS contributed 44,375 serving personnel, of which over 1,500 never returned and more than 1,000 were taken prisoner. In the course of their service they received over 150 decorations and were mentioned in despatches on 88 occasions. For gallantry during the 'Blitz' 54 awards were made by the King to LMS railwaymen.

MILITARY ASSISTANCE

This was afforded by the Royal Engineers at the time of the intensive bombing in 1940/1, rendering appreciable help in repairing air raid damage, usually consisting of 12 men with an officer in charge.

Such help was given at Willesden, Barking, Liverpool, Birmingham and Bristol. Unfortunately, no real forward planning could be carried out as these squads were all liable to recall by the Military Authorities at a moment's notice, which led to little reliance being placed on such assistance.

Scotland was more fortunate, with considerable assistance being given to the LMS over an extended period to provide many miles of new telephone circuits.

CIRCUIT CONSTRUCTION

New telephone circuits were provided to meet the Chief Operating Manager's requirements indicated by the fact that over 4,000 single wire miles of 200-lb copper wire (over 350 tons) were erected throughout the system, together with several miles of multi-core air-spaced cables. The gangs achieved nine to ten miles of single wire per week, a very creditable performance. Transport to the work sites and the feeding of the men were major wartime problems only solved by wholehearted co-operation of the gangs and their supervisors.

Assistance was rendered by squads of Royal Engineers from Edinburgh placed at the disposal of the LMS in connection with improved telephone facilities on the Highland Line. Work commenced in August 1941 with two Officers and sixty other ranks supplementing the railway gangs with the work proceeding in the following order:

Inverness to Wick and Thurso
Dingwall to Kyle of Lochalsh
Inverness to Keith–Aviemore and Perth
Perth to Aberdeen

The Highland scheme was completed in September 1942 when the party was split up, with 20 men being transferred to the LNER, the remainder assisting railway gangs in the erection of the new Perth–Balquhidder leg of the Perth–Oban circuit.

Assistance was also given by a number of men from the above squad with additional men from Edinburgh in connection with the work at Dunragit on the Dumfries–Stranraer Line.

AIR RAID PRECAUTIONS

Signal Boxes – Construction. Signal boxes were extremely vulnerable to bomb damage and blast, being constructed in many cases with a wood base and all had plenty of glass on the working floor level. Accordingly the Crewe Divisional Signal and Telegraph office, under H. E. Morgan, set about designing a signal box to withstand, as far as possible, the effects of enemy attack. The design utilised 14in brickwork walls with a reinforced concrete floor and roof as detailed in *Fig, 1* and *Plate 1*. A comprehensive article covering LMS signal boxes in wartime, by fellow LMS Society member Roy Anderson, appeared in *Backtrack* No. 1, Volume 12, 1998.

Signal Boxes – Lighting. It was laid down in May 1939 that signal box lighting was to be fully restricted and that no action was to be taken in regard to screening cabins beyond the provision of special lamps and lamp shades. These instructions proved to be too drastic, but it should be appreciated that to reduce the peacetime lighting of some 4000 signal boxes to wartime level in a few hours meant that clear instructions had to be given that could not be misinterpreted. There were three methods of illumination – electricity, gas and oil – with all signal boxes supplied with the necessary screens and lamps, etc, sometime prior to the outbreak of the war.

Plate 2. *The interior of Watford No. 1 signal box on 16th October 1939, showing the indoor air-raid shelter provided for the protection of signalmen as they were required to remain on duty at all times.*

COLLECTION ROY ANDERSON

Soon after the wartime lighting was introduced, signalmen in some boxes found difficulty in carrying out their duties, and in such cases, the box was visited and adjustments made to give the maximum amount of illumination the Government restrictions allowed. The statutory Rule and Order governing lighting was not issued by the Secretary of State for the Home Department until 1st September 1939, which stated that lights essential for the internal illumination of signal boxes be exempt from the general instruction with regard to the extinguishment of lights provided they complied with the following conditions:

1. That they were so screened that no light was thrown above the horizontal.
2. The intensity of illumination was reduced to the minimum necessary for the operation of signals.
3. That no light was thrown on any part of the window area of the box.

It was also agreed that the lights did not have to be extinguished during an air raid. There was also no need for the windows to be 'blacked out' or curtained for safety reasons. These restrictions made the lighting very poor and although experiments were made up to the end of 1942, no satisfactory solution was found.

However, in 1943 a system of indirect lighting proved successful, whereby lamps were fitted with metal bowls directing the light into the roof of the box giving a diffused light over the whole of the interior of the box. This enabled the signalman to see all his instruments, lever numbers, clock, etc, without strain, also without any glare the view through the windows was improved. Not all boxes were equipped with this method.

It was obviously essential that signalmen should remain at their posts at all times even though a raid might be in progress. To give signalmen the best possible protection, a steel shelter was provided that was placed on the working floor of the box, allowing the signalman to take cover at times when he was not concerned with traffic (*Plate 2*).

Signal Lights – Aerial observations were carried out in 1938 that established that semaphore signal lights were unlikely to give much assistance to enemy aircraft. The same could not be said for colour light signals when it was decreed that such signals should be provided with a hood 2ft 0in long which were all in place prior to the war commencing (*Fig. 2*). Banner

signals were also hooded, dependent on type. The very few oil-lit signals that were visible from the sea were also screened in various ways.

The very intense air raids in August and September 1940 caused the Government to think, that in spite of the hooding, colour light signals were aiding the Luftwaffe. To obviate this, switches were provided enabling the signalman to reduce the intensity of the lights by approximately 60% of the voltage and the light to 6% of normal, and turned to the 'dim' position at the commencement of the 'blackout' period, except when fog prevailed.

To safeguard against failure of the current supply to colour light installations, a number of mobile generating sets were stabled at strategical points throughout the LMS system, so that they could be taken to any place where a failure had occurred.

BOMB DAMAGE

The signalling system of the LMS was severely damaged on many occasions by Adolf Hitler and his Luftwaffe, or later by V1 and V2 rockets, and whilst this report only details major damage up to the middle of 1941, the LMS was only damaged on 347 occasions from the end of 1941 onwards compared with 1716 times before that date.

With the Battle of Britain won, the Blitz was virtually over by the middle of 1941, after which bombing was considerably reduced with the Germans relying latterly on V1 and V2 flying bombs and rockets, which, being centred on London, left the LMS, as a whole, largely out of range (see *Appendix E*).

Again it cannot be overstressed the huge part played by the railways in maintaining the war effort and the tremendous

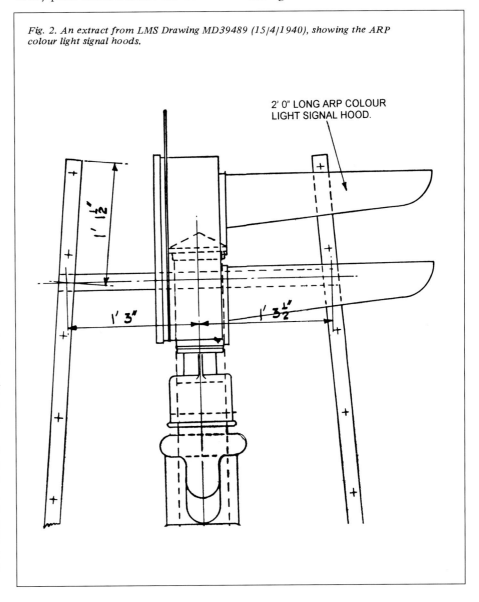

Fig. 2. An extract from LMS Drawing MD39489 (15/4/1940), showing the ARP colour light signal hoods.

2' 0" LONG ARP COLOUR LIGHT SIGNAL HOOD.

1' 3"

1' 3½"

Rail 197 - 201 COMs
Wartime Reports.

DATES OF ENEMY AIR RAIDS OVER SPECIFIED AREAS (MINOR RAIDS EXCLUDED).
(Day raids shewn 7th, etc. Night raids shewn 15/16, etc.)

APPENDIX 'C'.

	London Area.	Thames Estuary.	Birmingham and Coventry.	Manchester.	Liverpool and Birkenhead.	Leeds.	Sheffield.	Swansea.	Bristol.	Clydeside.
1940.										
June.	—	—	—	—	—	—	—	—	—	—
July.	—	—	—	—	—	—	—	—	—	—
August.	—	18th, 26th, 31st	25/26, 26/27	—	—	—	—	17/18	24/25, 13/14	—
September.	7th, 7/8, 8/9, 9/10, 10/11, 15/16, 17/18, 21/22, 25/26, 27/28, 28/29, 29/30, 31/1 Oct.	7th, 15th, 15/16, 27/28	—	—	4/5, 18/19, 21/22, 26/27, 29/30	—	—	1/2	—	—
October.	1/2, 2/3, 4/5, 5/6, 8/9, 9/10, 10/11, 13/14, 14/15, 15/16, 16/17, 19/20, 21/22, 23/24	14/15, 15/16	12/13, 16/17, 17/18, 18/19, 21/22, 24/25, 25/26, 26/27, 28/29, 31/1 Nov.	2/3, 7/8	11/12	—	—	—	—	—
November.	7/8, 15/16, 16/17	—	14/15, 19/20, 22/23	—	28/29	—	—	—	24/25	—
December.	3/4, 8/9, 29/30	—	3/4, 11/12	22/23, 23/24	20/21, 21/22, 22/23	—	12/13, 15/16	—	6/7	—
1941.										
January.	5/6, 11/12	12/13	—	—	9/10	—	—	—	16/17	—
February.	—	—	—	11/12	11/12	14/15	—	19/20, 20/21, 21/22	16/17	—
March.	8/9, 19/20	8/9, 19/20	—	—	12/13, 13/14, 14/15, 15/16, 26/27	—	—	—	11/12	13/14
April.	16/17, 17/18, 19/20	16/17, 19/20	8/9, 9/10, 10/11, 16/17	7/8	7 consecutive nights 1/2 to 7/8 inclusive.	—	—	—	—	7/8
May.	10/11	—	—	1/2	31/1 June.	—	—	—	—	5/6, 6/7
June.	—	—	—	—	—	—	—	—	—	—

Leicester.

effort made by staff to 'keep things running'.

The LMS suffered damage from enemy action in one form or another on over 2,000 occasions (see *Appendix C*) and the Signal and Telegraph Engineer's department was involved in a large percentage of them. Up to the end of 1943 there were 1,768 incidents involving damage to S&T equipment, of which 1,315 were directly caused by enemy action; the remainder, 453 cases, were due to various causes mentioned in the following summary:

	1939/40	1941	1942	1943	Total
Enemy action	599	665	41	10	1,315
British aircraft	9	15	11	25	60
Ack-ack gunfire	23	14	2	19	58
Barrage balloons coming adrift, trailing cables	177	108	21	28	334
British floating mine	–	–	–	1	1
Totals	**808**	**802**	**75**	**83**	**1,868**

Plate 3. *New Street No. 5 signal box following reconstruction.* V. PHILLIPS

The unusual floating mine incident was at Abergele, North Wales on 3rd January 1943. The mine exploded off the shore when the blast caused damage to the windows and roof of an adjacent signal box.

The majority of cases were of a minor nature, but there were several major incidents of enemy action, as shown in the brief account that follows with rather more details in the case of Birmingham (19/10/1940) and Manchester (23/12/1940).

18th August 1940 Shoeburyness
Two high explosive (HE) bombs dropped, one close to the station signal box and the other on the nearby permanent way. The box was practically demolished and all communications completely severed. The signalman was killed, this being war fatality number one on the LMS.

7th/8th September, 1940, London Area – London–Tilbury Section
The raid commenced at 5pm on the evening of the 7th when extensive damage was caused by HE and incendiary bombs. Signalling suffered considerable damage at several places throughout the Tilbury Section, generally to signal box structures, electrical signalling equipment, power cables and overhead lines of communication, much of which was completely destroyed. The Skinner Street linemen's Depot was burnt out.

13th October 1940, Birkenhead, Green Lane Junction
Four bombs were dropped (one delayed action) around the junction box that was wrecked. All block telegraph and telephone communications were severed and there was extensive damage to the permanent way, blocking all running lines. By 4.30pm the up fast line was re-opened for single line working and during the day communications were temporarily restored.

16th October 1940, London St. Pancras Station
The St. Pancras Junction and Station boxes were damaged by a land mine during the early morning. The relay apparatus and battery huts, with all their contents such as rectifiers and transformers were destroyed. The Lineman's Depot with almost all contents was also destroyed, as well as a bracket signal.

16th October 1940, Birmingham (New Street)
New Street No. 5 signal box was practically destroyed by a direct hit by an HE bomb about 8pm. The signal box was 76'3" long by 12'0" wide by 8'0" elevation, with a cellar 7'3" below rail level to accommodate the locking. It was fitted with a 153 lever Webb tumbler frame, the cellar and lower storey constructed of brickwork with a wooden superstructure from the working floor level. Virtually the whole of the brickwork of the lower storey was demolished, the blast destroying about forty levers, instrument shelf, block instruments, telephones, batteries, relays, etc, and damaging the wood portion beyond repair.

The following morning arrangements were made for complete possession of the running lines and debris amounting to forty wagon loads were cleared away; coincident with this an adjacent signal linesman's room was fitted up as a temporary block post by the provision of the required block instruments and field telephones.

It was decided to demolish the remaining portion of the brick lower storey and to use two of the ARP 43'3" emergency signal boxes, one being obtained from St. Helens and the other from Stafford Stores. On 17th these were loaded up and arrived, one on the same day and the other by special train early next morning. The variation in the overall length necessitated altering the corner and intermediate posts to suit, also the flooring to suit the Webb frame to which forty new levers were added, the whole frame being relocked.

The Crewe construction gang commenced on the rebuilding of the cellar portion of the old box to form the foundation for the new all-timber structure and the general work of construction continued from daylight to dark each day.

On the 20th a start was made on erecting the first half of the wood superstructure which had meanwhile been altered in

APPENDIX 'E'.

DAMAGES, BLOCKAGES AND CASUALTIES AS A RESULT OF ENEMY ACTION, 1939 - 1945.

(A) Damages and Blockages.

	1939.	1940.	1941.	1942.	1943.	1944.	1945.	Total.
(1) Number of occasions damage was caused.	Nil.	1,140	576	70	24	224	29	2,063
(2) Number of occasions running lines were obstructed.	Nil.	447	204	26	5	35	8	725
(3) Length of time lines were blocked.		Hrs.	Hrs.	Hrs.	Hrs.	Hrs.	Hrs.	Hrs. Hrs.
	Nil.	43,999	92,133	6,497	99	638	98	143,464

(B) Analysis of number of incidents.

Area.	Number of Incidents.	Percentage to Total.
London	593	28.7
Thames Estuary (East of Bromley)	188	9.1
Coventry, Birmingham, Wolverhampton.	277	13.4
Manchester	74	3.6
Liverpool and Merseyside.	269	13.1
Clydeside	60	2.9
Rest of England and Wales.	592	28.7
Rest of Scotland.	10	.5
	2,063	100.0

(C) Analysis of Damage caused by Flying Bombs and Rockets.

	Flying Bombs.	Rockets.	Total.
London.	32 (6)	23 (6)	55
Thames Estuary.	86 (9)	17 (2)	103
Elsewhere	11	1	12
	129	41	170

Figures in parenthesis indicate direct hits on Railway.

(D) Casualties - Killed and Injured.

	1939.		1940.		1941.		1942.		1943.		1944.		1945.		Total.	
	K.	I.	K.	I.	K.	I.	K.	I.	K.	I.	K.	I.	K.	I.	K.	I.
Passengers.	Nil		10	28	6	10	Nil.		Nil.		-	70	1	30	17	138
Railway Staff) on duty.)	Nil		27	281	21	125	-	13	Nil.		1	122	2	26	51	567
∅ Other Persons	Nil		1	10	2	8	Nil.		Nil.		1	29	Nil		4	47
Total :	Nil		38	319	29	143	-	13	Nil.		2	221	3	56	72	752

K. - Killed.   I. - Injured.

∅ Persons on business at stations, Home Guards, etc.

APPENDIX E – LMS damage, blockages and casualties 1939 to 1945.

height and also made suitable to join up with the second half. The first half, including the floor, was finished and the roof sheeted over as a temporary measure on the 22nd. The remaining half was erected in 10'0" sections each day, commencing the next morning, to suit the progress with the brickwork of the cellar. The final stage was erected on 26th, the floor completed and the roof sheeted over the following day, when all the window sashes were fixed and gas lighting installed.

The points were then coupled up to the levers which remained without interlocking, the block instruments and telephones installed, and the signalman returned to the box at 6pm on the 27th, eleven days after the mishap. Complete restoration of all interlocking was effected at 1pm on 7th November, but the roof was not finished and slated until the 19th November (*Plate 3*).

During the period of disconnection, traffic operations were carried on by ground staff who operated the points and flagged trains under the instructions of the signalman in the temporary block post.

Communications suffered severely, the District Control Office and Telegraph Office being completely destroyed, necessitating operating from the Shelter Control Office. Ultimately, as previously stated, new offices were provided. At Birmingham Lawley Street, prompt action by the S&T Engineer's staff enabled the automatic switchboard and associated equipment to be protected from extensive damage by fire and water, and the apparatus was ultimately overhauled and reinstated. All line cables leading into New Street Station and Lawley Street were also destroyed, involving extensive renewals.

14th/15th November, 1940. Raid on Coventry Area

The LMS had its share of the bombing during this major raid and at various points received such a hammering as to bring operations in the area almost to a standstill. Many bombs were dropped about the station, yards, and the running lines and, along with the rest of the service, the S&T equipment suffered badly. A large number of signal boxes were structurally damaged together with the signalling connections and apparatus but fortunately in no case was there a 'knock-out' of a signal box as an operating unit. Considerable lengths of overhead pole routes were brought down and cable work destroyed, causing serious interference with communications.

19th/20th November, 1940. Birmingham Area

As with the Coventry raids, the Birmingham raids were very severe, causing considerable destruction throughout the railway in the Birmingham area. Signal boxes and signalling equipment with cable routes and overhead telegraph wires received considerable damage, causing signalling operations and telegraphic and telephonic communications to be put out of use.

22nd/23rd December, 1940. Manchester Area

In these heavy raids the railway was severely bombed and signal and telegraphs received considerable damage. A number of signal boxes were damaged chiefly through broken windows. In two cases only was damage severe, the Salford Incline Box being completely demolished and Ordsall Lane No. 4 having the upper portion destroyed by fire. Damage was done to signalling plant, but it was more serious to S&T equipment in connection with communications apparatus and wires. At Manchester Exchange Station serious effect upon all communications was caused by the destruction of the whole of the cables and wires attached to the wall of the station buildings that were completely burnt out. On 23rd December Victoria Station received the brunt of the attack, and buildings, including the Divisional Control Office, were destroyed, the whole of the telephonic and telegraphic apparatus, including loud-speaker equipment, being destroyed. This was a major disaster and although the personnel were safe in the shelter, the structure was shaken and serious flooding resulted. All line cables and terminations were destroyed by fire, but skeleton contact with outside Control Offices was quickly given, and all Control circuits were restored by temporary cables within a few days. Improvisation of the temporary Control Office, restoration of equipment and cables to enable the shelter to be re-occupied, and finally provision of a new Control Office with the Shelter as standby, involved a large amount of work at a critical period.

Destruction of Manchester Exchange Station and the heavy damage in the area resulted in the destruction of many miles of multi-core cable and open line wire, and the restoration work was made more difficult by the simultaneous destruction of all the emergency cable stocks in the Manchester Area.

11th December, 1940. Perry Barr

A land mine was dropped on the embankment about 30 yards from the North Junction signal box, destroying the lower brickwork and badly damaging the upper wood structure. Considerable damage was done to the lever frame and apparatus, also the block instruments and telephones. The work of erecting a temporary block post was immediately taken in hand and brought into use on the afternoon of 12th December.

12th and 15th December, 1940. Sheffield

During these raids Sheffield South No. 1 signal box was completely demolished by blast and subsequent fire, along with the interlocking frame of 68 levers, and apparatus, comprising the whole of the block instruments, repeaters, indicators and telephones. South No. 2 box had all windows and the roof and timber sheeting blown out, and the whole of the switchboard cabling to the two position manual switchboard at Sheffield Station Telegraph Office had to be renewed on site, service being maintained whilst the wiring was dealt with (*Plates 4–7*).

20th to 23rd December, 1940. Liverpool Area

The LMS suffered extensive damage during these raids and much damage was done to signalling. A number of signal boxes were damaged, two beyond repair, along with the apparatus and connections therein. Signals, outside connections, overhead wires and cables were all affected. The Signal Stores at Bank Hall received damage to the roof and the telephone exchange and telephones in the Canada Dock Warehouse, which burnt out, were completely destroyed.

15th and 16th January, 1941. Derby Station

Derby Station received a direct hit and damage was caused to the windows of the Station 'A' and Engine Sidings No. 2 signal boxes. Nos. 4 and 6 platform colour light signals were destroyed and damage was caused to crossover points between Nos. 3 and 4 platforms. Cables from the station to the Locomotive Works were damaged by blast and wiring circuits to the colour light signals referred to were destroyed. Damage was also sustained to the loud speakers and some open wires were brought down.

16th and 17th January, 1941. Avonmouth

Three boxes were more or less seriously damaged – Dock Junction, Sidings and

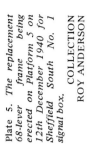

Plate 5. The replacement frame being erected on Platform 5 on 12th December 1940 for Sheffield South No. 1 signal box.
COLLECTION
ROY ANDERSON

Plate 4. Sheffield South No. 1 signal box was completely destroyed on 12th December 1940 and is seen here in the process of being rebuilt.
COLLECTION ROY ANDERSON

Plate 6. *Sheffield South No. 2 signal box on 12th December 1940 following an enemy air-raid, the box having suffered severe bomb damage with all the wood panels blown out together with windows and roof tiles.*
COLLECTION
ROY ANDERSON

Plate 7. *Sheffield South No. 2 as rebuilt, taken in 1963, with Sheffield South No. 1 in the background, which was completely destroyed in the same raid.*
MIKE KING

Dock station boxes. A gantry signal was destroyed, also signal connections and a bracket signal damaged.

8th/10th April, 1941. Coventry
The telephone exchange was completely destroyed and Nos. 2, 3 and 4 signal boxes and connections damaged together with pole routes.

8th/10th April, 1941. Birmingham
The windows of eight signal boxes were damaged. One signal gantry was demolished and two other signals blown down. At New Street all communications were cut.

It was on April 16th 1941 that the President of the LMS Railway, Josiah Stamp, First Baron Stamp of Shortlands, together with his wife, Olive Jessie and their eldest son Wilfred Carlyle Stamp were killed in their London home by enemy action.

17th April, 1941. London Area
The signal box at Haggerston was seriously damaged, also four others to a lesser extent. A signal gantry at Haggerston was demolished. Aerial wires were brought down at several places. At River Rom a District train (empty) received a direct hit and rested on the cables, that fortunately did not affect their working.

19th/20th April, 1941. London Area
Nine signal boxes received structural damage and broken windows. Aerial wires were brought down and cables damaged at many places. At New Inn Yard signal box, all block and other instruments were put out of order. Plaistow traction sub-station was damaged, putting out of use the signalling equipment.

26th April and 26th May, 1941. Liverpool Area
A total of some eighty locations (offices, signal boxes, etc.) were damaged, main multi-core cables and all open wires being down in numerous sections. Twenty signal boxes received damage, with that to Bootle Station and Dale Lane No. 2 being considerable. Liverpool Exchange 'B' box and gantry were badly damaged by fire.

The control Office at Aintree, Telegraph Office at Liverpool Exchange Station and the Telephone Exchange at Canada Dock were demolished, a temporary board installed at Canada Dock again being destroyed in the later raid. The various Goods Offices and Station Telephone

Exchanges were interconnected by about fifty Post Office maintained tie lines, and, owing to the extensive damage suffered by the Post Office, chaotic conditions prevailed initially. It was only due to the provision of temporary tie lines by the S&T Engineer's Department over devious railway routes that skeleton intercommunication was afforded within a week or so.

At the board meeting held on 29th May 1941, (minute 4289) The Chairman, Sir Ernest Lemon, gave details of the damage done at Liverpool, Birmingham and elsewhere and 'explained the difficulty experienced in carrying out essential repairs owing to the Government's dilatory system of priorities and licences having regard to the vital nature of railway traffic in the country's war effort'. The Board authorized the Chairman to approach the Government with the object of overcoming avoidable delays.

5th to 7th May, 1941. Glasgow and Clydeside
Damage was caused to nine signal boxes, those at Greenock Central and Gourock No. 1 of a serious nature. Aerial wires were brought down in many places, telephone communication and block working between Langbank and Port Glasgow and between Wemyss Bay Junction and Greenock were made inoperative, necessitating all trains being run on a time interval.

10th and 11th May, 1941. London Area
Seven signal boxes were damaged, that at Poplar seriously so. Signals and signal and point connections were damaged, aerial wires brought down and cables destroyed with damage at several other places.

Appendix 'C' extracted from The LMS Operating Manager's Report 1939–1943 (PRO Rail 418/197) summarizes the major air raids over this period.

Appendix 'E' extracted from The LMS Operating Manager's Report for 1945 (PRO Rail 418/201) tabulates the 2,063 times the LMS was damaged by enemy action throughout the Second World War.

RESTORATION
The above instances of major damage that were incurred at the main centres was typical of the widespread destruction that affected hundreds of other centres during the 'Blitz' period. The immense amount

of restoration work involved to preserve continuity of communication services threw a terrific strain on the department's labour and material resources, and the successful carrying out of the work was a magnificent achievement on the part of all S&T staff.

Restoration work had to continue long after the actual event, as repairs, initially of a temporary nature, had to be made permanent later, and indeed had priority over everything else. Work was undertaken with the utmost expediency, often under very difficult and dangerous conditions with an 'alert' still in progress, which, under 'blackout' conditions, made it a matter of wonderment that at times communications were restored before the 'all clear' was sounded.

The provision of new, and the preservation of existing services by the S&T Engineer's staff facilitated in no small measure the task of the Operating Department, and the Chief Operating Manager's successful and efficient traffic working was adequate testimony to the work performed by the S&T Department..

ROAD TRANSPORT
Prior to the war the S&T department possessed no road motor vehicles, in fact arising out of the rail and road controversy of pre-war days, it was a matter of personal pride, not to say prejudice, to make the minimum use of road services, but the war altered that viewpoint and experience gained since 1939 made road transport essential.

Road transport proved to be a highly effective time and money saver, as with a restricted wartime train service, not to mention no service at all due to enemy action, the movement of men and materials by road proved to be of paramount importance.

The first vehicle was a 10 cwt. Fordson motor van delivered to the Barking Depot for use throughout that area which was somewhat remote from the rest of the system (*Plate 8*). Following the restriction of train services, a further van was obtained for the Rugby Depot which proved to be such a valuable aid that as soon as they could be obtained, similar vans were supplied to Manchester, Sheffield, Chester, Bristol and Glasgow. Additionally, vans of 30 cwt capacity were supplied to Stoke, Warrington, Bedford and Perth.

Watford Depot was of such importance to the London Area that a 3 ton lorry was substituted for the 10 cwt van. Each van was fitted with tool cupboards, equipped with essential tools and a short ladder. A suitable man was trained to drive by the Road Motor Department.

The vans proved to be a very great asset in moving men and materials from place to place, especially in country districts where the train service was restricted. In the case of air raid damage, it was possible to commence, and at times complete, repairs long before men would have been available by train service. In connection with new works, the maximum amount of time could be spent on the job without it being necessary to have regard to the timing of the last return train, the coming of darkness being the deciding factor, thereby hastening completion of the work and generally effecting a considerable saving in travelling time and/or lodging expenses.

Plate 9 portrays a trailer fitted out as a mobile workshop.

In view of the possible necessity for transporting heavy stores and men in an emergency, arrangements were made with the Chief Operating Manager and the Chief Commercial Manager that the S&T department had an A1 priority call on the

Plate 8. A 10cwt Fordson van, fleet No. 175-S at Radcliffe, Manchester on 2nd December 1940. COLLECTION NELSON TWELLS

Plate 9. A trailer fitted out as a mobile workshop (No. 1MWS), complete with blacksmith's hearth, jacks, vices, portable generator, grinding wheel, etc. COLLECTION NELSON TWELLS

services of a heavy motor lorry and driver at thirteen specified centres. During the heavy 'Blitz' on Liverpool, this assistance proved invaluable for men as well as material, as in various directions transport had entirely broken down, with the lorry collecting the gangs in the morning and returning them home at night. Road bolster vehicles were also similarly used for the transport of stores of unusual dimensions such as signal posts and telegraph poles.

An appreciable number of supervisory staff possessed their own motor cars and, when petrol restrictions came into force, such cars were maintained by the Company and run on petrol drawn from the Company's supply solely for use on Departmental business. In some cases, cars were supplied by the Company for key personnel.

RAIL TRANSPORT

Following the severe damage by enemy action in the early part of the war and more particularly that at Liverpool, the LMS set up a system whereby a dining and kitchen car coupled to a 3rd class sleeping coach were stabled at eight places throughout the system to accommodate and feed men hurriedly called away from their home depot in connection with repair of serious damage necessitating continuous effort during the hours of daylight.

A temporary telephone was fitted in each of the kitchen cars to enable the number of meals required and the time of the men's arrival to be advised. A stock of non-perishable food was kept permanently in the cars for this purpose. In addition to this, four mobile canteens were provided for emergency repair gangs of the Chief Civil Engineer and the S&T Engineer dis-

pensing hot soup and tea as well as corned beef, bread and margarine (*Plate 10*).

These canteens were under the control of the District Civil Engineers and located at Northampton, Walsall, Blackburn and Glasgow. They were available for despatch to any point required, either by road or rail according to the circumstances, crane power being required at the destination to lift the canteen off the carriage truck or road motor trailer.

For normal work necessitating men living away from home for an extended period, in view of the difficulty of finding lodgings under war conditions, the use of dormitory coaches was considerably extended. Prior to the war the use of such vehicles was confined to Scotland where, north of Perth, habitations were scattered. The five pre-war vehicles were extended to seven and in view of the isolated nature

Plate 10. *A Commer 15cwt van, fleet No. 178-S, fitted out as a mobile canteen, with one allocated to each of the four Divisional Civil Engineers.*
COLLECTION NELSON TWELLS

of the surrounding country, the men's evening amusement was catered for by the provision of dart boards, cards and games.

South of the border, nineteen dormitory coaches were provided by the conversion of holiday caravan coaches, each having provision for eighteen men per coach. These vehicles served a very useful purpose when so many Government works were in hand, but they had the disadvantage of requiring siding accommodation that on occasions meant a walk of several miles to and from the site of the work.

Portable huts were provided on the Western Division, built in sections and secured by lynch pins enabling erection to be completed within an hour. Each hut housed eight men and contained bunks hinged from the wall and swung out of the way during daytime, leaving room for a table and forms for mess purposes. These huts proved to be of great value when constructing telephone lines as they accommodated a construction gang and could be moved along as the work progressed and so provided the maximum time on the job.

Difficulties continually arose in connection with rations, with schemes being approved and accepted in certain areas and being turned down by Local Food Officers in other areas, and it was not until September 1943 that the Ministry of Food approved a scheme that was satisfactory to both the men and the Company.

In pre-war days most S&T gangs were provided with rail vans in which were stored and transported all necessary tools, ladders, ropes, etc. These vans, when placed in an adjacent siding, could also be used as a workshop and as a place where meals could be taken under cover when other accommodation was not available. The stock of forty-nine vans was augmented by a further sixteen to cater for the additional gangs necessitated by war conditions.

EMERGENCY MEASURES

During the heavy 'Blitz' period in 1940/41, an organisation was set up at Headquarters Watford and other key centres whereby staff would be available throughout the twenty-four hours to collect, and convey immediately by telephone to those concerned, all available details of railway damage arising from enemy action, also to go out to the scene of the damage to gain an idea of what was required by way of men and materials to make the necessary repairs as soon as daylight returned. To this end, every Area Technical Assistant was equipped with a Post Office telephone, with certain Chief Officers as well as the Executive registered with the Post Office as being entitled to special priority calls.

In most instances, this emergency organisation was joint between the Chief Civil Engineer and the S&T Engineer with alternate turns being worked by their respective staffs. In view of the expense involved, this organisation was cancelled during the comparatively quiet periods in 1942/43 but could be reinstated at very short notice if circumstances warranted it.

At the Board meeting held on 24th October 1940, minute 4170 approved the 'establishment of special repair department recruited from all districts for restoration of railway property damaged by enemy bombing'.

In 1940 a pocket-size pamphlet was issued in which the full emergency organisation was set out, enabling those responsible to have all the required information to hand at any time by day or night. This was amplified in 1942 with a supplement based on experience gained, with both issues kept up to date as alterations took place.

MAJOR NEW WORKS

At the outbreak of the war, the LMS was committed to certain new works that, for various reasons, could not be deferred indefinitely and, by arrangement with the Ministry of War Transport, were proceeded with providing the war effort was not hindered. These were:

Rugby – Colour light signalling and track circuiting of the main running lines, the purpose of which was to reduce the headway through Rugby from five to three minutes.

Crewe – Colour light signalling and full track circuiting, together with the provision of two signal boxes built to the Air Raid Precaution specification.

Wigan – Resignalling with colour lights and full track circuiting when three new electro mechanical signal boxes replaced twelve mechanical boxes.

Camden to Sudbury – Colour light signalling and track circuiting of running lines to gain improved headway between these points.

These schemes will all be dealt with in detail in *LMS Journal* later.

Signal Renewals

These were ongoing all the year round with the Sighting Committee continuously employed viewing all signals reported for renewal, recommending any desirable alteration in the site, construction or height of the replacements. This work came under the Chief Operating Manager (COM), with all recommendations reviewed at HQ by the COM and S&T Engineer.

The pre-war target for renewals was in the region of one thousand per annum. During the war only the most urgent cases could be dealt with, which left a heavy programme of deferred work awaiting the cessation of hostilities as follows:

Signal renewals – all types

Year	1939	1940	1941	1942	1943	Total Deficit
Completed	864	500	494	621	892	
Outstanding Balance	136	500	506	379	106	1,629

Many signals had their life extended by heavy timber slabbing or 'grandfathering', additional guying or even heavy props produced from old telegraph poles.

Aerial Route – Renewals

Continuous attention was required to pole routes and a heavy programme of deferred work built up. The problem was different from signal renewal in that a pole line being continuous, it was possible to extend the life by dealing only with the weakest link, concentrating on the maintenance of the most important circuits. This was not the ideal policy but the force of circumstances left no option, leaving heavy arrears to be dealt with later:

	Authorised for 1939	Completed 1939 to 1943 inc.	Average per annum
Poles	2,820	3,015	603
Arms	26,750	32,620	6,523
Stay wire – cwts.	2,055	2,895	579
Iron wire – cwts.	8,040	13,950	2,790
Copper wire – cwts.	1,685	3,090	618
Insulators	55,570	99,100	19,820
Insulator Bolts	69,700	112,150	22,430

From the foregoing one can readily appreciate the problems building up on the railways of Britain following cessation of hostilities by way of a tremendous backlog of maintenance. This article just refers to signals and telegraph lines, but to this must be added permanent way, rolling stock, locomotives and building maintenance, etc. Small wonder the railways took several years to get back to anything approaching the pre-war standard and doubtless the Government failed on its promises of paying for the wartime services rendered, just as it did following the first World War.

RE-USE OF MATERIALS

Board minute 4124 dated 25th July 1940 included a report by Sir Harold Hartley, dealing with redundant assets and the salvaging and re-use of what in pre-war days would have been scrap. All the LMS Works were involved and photographs included of what had been achieved. The S&T Department had several examples, one of which was a single post signal – see *Plate 11*.

APPRECIATION

The Board meeting on 26th September 1940 requested the Chairman Lord Stamp to convey to Mr Wallace (Chief Civil Engineer) and Mr Bound (Signal and Telegraph Engineer) together with their staff, the Board's appreciation of their fine work in repairing air raid damage and keeping lines open for traffic.

FINALLY

The War ended in Europe on 8th May 1945 and the first Board meeting following victory was held on 24th May, when an address was sent to Their Majesties as follows – Board Minute 4937 with Sir Robert Burrows in the Chair, in the absence of The Hon. Lord Royden, C.H.

May it please Your Majesty,

The Directors of the LMS present their humble duty and ask permission to express to you on behalf of the stockholders and servants of the LMS Railway their sincere and respectful congratulations on the unconditional surrender of the common enemy on the Continent.

It is a matter of pride to all associated with the LMS Railway that under Your Majesty's Ministries, the Company has played no small part in helping to bring about a victorious end of the war.

Vast numbers of troops, ammunition and stores have been conveyed under conditions of exceptional difficulty; workshops created for the manufacture of rolling stock have been adapted to the construction of aeroplanes and the accoutrements of war; a large number of staff has been called to the colours and many others have been rostered for duty where their technical qualifications have been needed for the prosecution of the war.

In all their arduous efforts the spirits of all ranks have been heartened by the presence among them of Your Majesty and The Queen on the many occasions on which you have travelled over the LMS Railway, and it is the sincere and devout wish of all that you may be long spared to rule over an empire of peace.

The war against Japan ended on 13th August 1945, but with no Board meeting until 27th September, this event surprisingly received no mention.

Acknowledgements

W. J. Sadler, Roy Anderson, Vic Phillips, Mike King, Nelson Twells, The PRO Kew, *LMS at War* by G. C. Nash.

Plate 11. *An LMS single-post signal at Kentish Town on 17th May 1940 utilising a 5½in diameter ex locomotive smoke tube as the main stem with a 6½in diameter bottom portion of new material. It is understood that the post quickly deteriorated.*
NATIONAL RAILWAY MUSEUM
(DY27008)

Plate 12. *Vauxhall and Duddeston station, Birmingham, following the bombing on 1st November 1940. The view is from the down platform and shows the damage caused to structures and permanent way. Although signals or signal boxes may not have been directly damaged, it is likely that signal wires, point rodding, telegraph lines and track circuits would have required repair.*
COLLECTION
NELSON TWELLS

Plate 13. *Bomb damage at Highbury and Islington station, London, on the North London line. Whilst the electrified lines appear to have been undamaged, the cabling cleated to the retaining wall had clearly been affected and most probably track circuiting.*
COLLECTION NELSON TWELLS

Wilson Carter & Pearson Ltd.

Colliery Proprietors & Exporters of Cannel & Gas Coal,

Birmingham, 2. 5th July 1939.

Messrs. Lamont & Warne,

31/33, Coal Exchange, London, E.C.3.

We have this day **sold to** *you as follows :—*

Quantity . . .	100/150 (One hundred to one hundred and fifty) tons per week. (Colliery option)
Quality . . .	Grassmoor Coke Dust, as at present supplied.
Price . . .	6/6d (Six shillings and six pence) per ton loaded into wagons at Ovens.
Time of Delivery .	From 1st July to 31st December 1939.
Mode of Delivery .	As above.
Terms of Payment	Nett Cash Monthly.
Remarks . . .	For delivery to the Staveley Coal & Iron Company.

CONDITIONS OF SALE.

1.—Deliveries may be wholly or partially suspended during the whole or partial stoppage of work at the colliery from which the fuel contracted for is for the time being supplied, through strikes, lock-outs, or accidents of all kinds, or any other occurrence beyond the control of the Vendors.

2.—Suspended deliveries arising from any of the before-mentioned causes shall at the option of the Vendors, be delivered after the cause of stoppage has been removed at the Contract rate of delivery, and this Contract shall be extended to enable such suspended deliveries to be made.

3.—The failure of any one delivery not to vitiate or affect this Contract.

4.—If after the date of this Contract there shall be any increase or decrease in the Railway rate, the Contract price shall be increased or decreased in the same proportion.

5.—If the purchaser shall make default in any payment, or shall become subject to the Bankruptcy Law, or make a Deed of Assignment for the benefit of, or Composition with, his Creditors, the Vendors may at

This is an example of a typical contract for the supply of coke, negotiated by one of Birmingham's three major coal factors, Wilson, Carter and Pearson Ltd., for coke from the Grassmoor colliery to be sent to various depots of the Army.

COAL TRAFFIC IN THE BIRMINGHAM AREA
by KEITH TURTON
PART I – INTRODUCTION

IN *Midland Record No. 5* the extent, infrastructure, coal consumption, by-products and traffic generated, both inwards and outwards, by the City of Birmingham Gas Department was described in detail, together with the source of the raw materials which provided Britain's second city with its Town Gas for domestic lighting, heating and cooking, its street lighting and industry. It may have surprised some readers that a municipally-owned utility consumed annually (in the late 1930s) well over a million tons of coal a year and this required exceptional organisation and coordination with the LMS Railway Company for delivery.

Simultaneously, the same gasworks were responsible for the annual sale of over half a million tons of coke and by-products such as tar, pitch, sulphuric acid, creosote and chemical derivatives, which were distributed by rail as far away as Glasgow to manufacturers of timber preservatives, chemicals, dyestuffs, explosives, soap and fertiliser, all of which required a regular supply of incoming empty wagons which almost equalled the number that arrived at the gasworks loaded with coal.

Only the city and its nearby suburbs were supplied by the Birmingham gasworks. In addition to this large undertaking there were, within the counties of Warwickshire, Worcestershire and Staffordshire, which now form the administrative district of the West Midlands, several other local gasworks, two large enough to carbonise over 100,000 tons of coal a year (Coventry and Wolverhampton) and at least three that used half that amount (Walsall, Smethwick and West Bromwich).

All these works obtained their coal from the same mining areas as those supplying the City of Birmingham, and with very few exceptions, all required the services of the LMS to transport the coal from colliery to gasworks. They also produced coke and by-products that were sold to many local companies whose names may still be well-known in the area; companies such as Chance and Hunt, Midland Tar Distillers, Brotherton Ltd., and Tarmac Ltd, were all supplied by the Birmingham gasworks.

In the days when privately-owned wagons, boldly displaying on their sides the names of coal factors and colliery companies, were to be found by the hundreds of thousands across the country, they identified, when owned by colliery companies, the origin of their contents. Many writers and historians have questioned the presence of wagons belonging to, in particular, Derbyshire and Yorkshire collieries, in mining strongholds of the midlands. The simple explanation is that they were delivering gas coal to the various works and, to a lesser extent, foundry and furnace coke to industry.

It must be stressed that coal mined in Leicestershire, South Derbyshire, Warwickshire and Cannock Chase, fine as it was for household and some industrial use and distributed to many parts of the country, was totally unsuitable for gas production. This created substantial business for the LMS, which in the mid-1930s, from its own records, was carrying some eighty-seven million tons of coal a year, of which, as near as can be calculated, included slightly less than three million tons of gas coal from, to a lesser extent the Potteries, but daily, in several trainloads, from Nottinghamshire, Derbyshire and Yorkshire into Birmingham, the Black Country and beyond.

For those whose interest lies in industrial history, and particularly that of Birmingham and the Black Country and highlighting its industrial railways, it is worthwhile to seek out a copy of *Industrial Railways of the West Midlands*, by R. E. Shill (Industrial Railway Society 1992). In this book, in addition to gasworks, power stations, brickworks, quarries, steelworks, iron foundries, glassworks, collieries and large manufacturing plants, a comprehensive survey is given describing all the industry that operated their own private railways. In addition, there were many other companies that received considerable quantities of coal; they owned their own private sidings that were connected to the mainline railway company but they did not own their own locomotives and relied upon the railway company to shunt the inwards and outwards traffic. Although this book gives no indication of the amount of coal consumed, it is indicative of the destination of coal used in Birmingham every day by industry, for almost all of these plants used coal as fuel.

But only a proportion of industry enjoyed the convenience of its own railway sidings; a lot of those smoking chimneys would have been fuelled by coal brought by first, horse and dray, then steam lorries or traction engines, and finally by motor lorry, to the factory premises from a convenient railway siding. Even some large consumers, such as the gasworks at Adderley Street, Birmingham, one at Dudley, and some of the smaller gasworks, had no railway facilities and relied on road transport from a nearby siding for their supplies.

The total tonnage of coal consumed by the various users will probably never be known. Neither will the percentage of the tonnage that could have been broken down into the various categories of consumer be discovered; as far as I am aware, no statistics are known to have been recorded, and if they were, they have not survived. However, records of many of the gas companies were preserved and, although scattered all over the country, sometimes in inappropriate repositories and infrequently recorded in the solitary trade journal, it has been possible to estimate with reasonable accuracy the volume of gas coal being delivered into the Birmingham area, and that which passed through en route to consumers in other parts of the country.

Many gasworks were owned by the local municipal authority, whose interest in utilities extended also to pumping stations for water and sewage, and later to generating stations for the supply of electricity. Here, the importance of the canal network should never be underestimated. Before the coming of the railway, it was the canal that opened up the midlands as an industrial entrepôt that encompassed the entire planet as customers for the output from its factories. That the canal outstripped the railway in tonnage supplied to some industries and utilities is confirmed by the fact that the entire fuel supply for the Walsall Corporation power station at Birchills was delivered from Cannock Chase and Warwickshire collieries in narrow boats and butty barges until the late 1940s, whilst supply to the Ockers Hill power station, near West Bromwich, was delivered by water until 1943 and most of that for the more substantial generating stations at Wolverhampton and Coventry also arrived by canal.

One of the few statistics to draw on is the tonnage carried in 1914 by the various canals of the Birmingham Canal Navigation system, which encompassed most canals serving the Black Country and Birmingham itself. They record that three-and-a-half million tons of coal was carried into the overall area, all but three-quarters of a million tons for industry, described ambiguously as 'Works Supply'. The latter would include any sent to pumping works, gas works and power stations.

It was the practice initially to build gasworks beside one of the many canals that threaded the Black Country, antedating the railway by several decades. Thus we find that the Swan Village works of the City of Birmingham was established in 1829 beside the Birmingham Canal Navigation, allowing coal to be delivered direct. It was not until 1873 that a siding was laid into the works, although coal had been delivered exclusively by rail since at least 1862, being transported from the nearest suitable station, then Great Bridge on the LNWR South Staffordshire branch, where coal from the Staveley Company's pits near Chesterfield could have been sent via the Midland Railway as far as Wychnor Junction, on the Birmingham and Derby line and then via the LNWR line between Lichfield and Walsall.

This was a typical example that was repeated throughout the Black Country for the supply of gas coal. There were two reasons why traffic was switched away from the canals to the railways: (1) The canals were incapable of maintaining the tonnage required to keep the fast expanding gasworks in production and for several weeks during the winter they were usually frozen over or 'stopped', and (2) There were very few collieries in the immediate vicinity that could supply suitable coal for gasworks by canal, the nearest were in the Potteries around Stoke on Trent; these shipments came via the Trent and Mersey Canal. There were collieries in the Erewash Valley that supplied gas coal and shipments came via the Erewash Canal, a slow and laborious route via Long Eaton and then along the Trent and Mersey Canal, the Coventry Canal, the Wyrley and Essington Canal and finally the Birmingham Canal Network. This was, as will be explained later, an ideal method for coal travelling to the generating stations and water-works, but for gas coal the coming of the rail-way was a necessity.

In an earlier instalment of this survey, published in *Midland Record 20*, I described the immense volume of coal required to keep Birmingham's five (later four) gasworks working, and the origins of the coal suggesting the routes for each of the three thousand wagons a week that transported gas coal from up to thirty different collieries located in the north of Nottinghamshire, Derbyshire and in Yorkshire, and lesser quantities from North Wales and the Potteries to the Birmingham area.

It is appropriate, therefore, to continue a survey of Birmingham's coal traffic, culled from the resources available, by completing the section on gas coal, and then examining coal for electricity and other municipal purposes.

GAS COAL

Based on recorded contracted coal purchases in the late 1930s, it was relatively easy to calculate the amount of coal carbonised for most of the gasworks in an area extending slightly beyond the accepted boundaries of the West Midlands. The coal purchased for this area, which includes Coventry, Tamworth, Nuneaton, Lichfield, Rugeley, Cannock Chase, Kidderminster, Redditch and Leamington Spa, totalled three-quarters of a million tons annually, ranging from 150,000 tons used by Coventry to small operations like Chasetown, which used only two thousand tons. However, it should be noted this tonnage of coal was in addition to requirements of the City of Birmingham Gas Works. Finally, we must not overlook an estimated half-million tons sent from Notts, Derbyshire and Yorkshire collieries to Shropshire, Hereford, Worcestershire, Gloucestershire, Wiltshire, Devon, Somerset, Bristol and South Wales gasworks, which largely travelled through the Birmingham area.

It is reasonable to calculate that the LMS carried 95% of this amount; some would be hauled by the Company for the entire journey

between colliery and consumer, while a considerable amount would be transferred to the Great Western at Bordesley exchange siding on the GWR London to Birmingham line. These calculations would indicate that about two and three-quarter million tons were carried annually by the LMS, mostly on the main cross-country line from Toton via Burton and Tamworth to Washwood Heath Marshalling

Yard for re-marshalling prior to being hauled to its final destination, although further remarshalling for some traffic would take place. For example, West of England traffic would be worked through to Westerleigh near Bristol and re-marshalled again before being worked to its final destination or transferred to the GWR. Some traffic was transferred from the LMS Midland to Western divisions at Wichnor

A transfer coal train from the LNWR South Staffordshire line via Dudley, arriving at the GWR and ex-LNWR junction at Dudley. The line to the left was the GWR branch from Stourbridge Junction to Wolverhampton with the LNWR Dudley goods station and sidings in the background.
COUNTY BOROUGH OF DUDLEY, MUSEUMS AND LIBRARIES SERVICE

Junction, south of Burton-on-Trent and travelling via Lichfield to reach destinations on the former LNWR or to exchange sidings with the GWR.

These assumptions are based upon the fact that the LMS, as the railway where the traffic originated, hauled the coal for the maximum possible distance before handing it over to another railway company, in this case the Great

Western. It is also possible that the route taken was influenced by the policy of maximising the revenue that came to the LMS by ensuring that as many miles as possible were over LMS lines.

The totals mentioned above represent about 52,000 tons a week or 5,500 wagonloads based upon an average load of almost 9½ tons per wagon, which may be slightly on the high side. This would mean over a hundred mineral trains

a week. As an example of this traffic, the Windsor Street works of the City of Birmingham Gas Department, situated on a mineral branch of the ex-LNWR near Aston station, received seven trainloads a day made up of loaded and empty wagons, the latter being sent by their owners to be loaded with coke and by-products from the works. Some gasworks also used canal transport for coke and

A typical industrial scene at the Mond Industrial Gas plant at Tipton. The works locomotive Lance can be seen with two coke wagons belonging to T. L. Hale (Tipton) Ltd. of Dudley Port and a wagon from the Ansley Hall Colliery near Nuneaton.

AUTHOR'S COLLECTION

this continued until well into the 1950s. The gasworks in the area where records were available for study are listed below.

BILSTON
The gasworks were located on the former Great Western Railway near Bilston station and consumed annually 25,000 tons, all but 3,000 tons coming from north Staffordshire, via the ex-LNWR lines and Bushbury Junction, with Shelton being the biggest supplier. The balance came from Derbyshire. Most of the trade was handled by local coal factors.

CANNOCK, HEDNESFORD AND DISTRICT GAS CO.
The works were located at Cannock on the former LNWR and supplied several towns in Cannock Chase, as indicated by their title. Twelve thousand tons of coal a year were consumed, coming from north Staffordshire (5,000), Derbyshire (3,000) and Yorkshire (4,000). The principal supplier was the Norton and Biddulph Colliery near Stoke-on-Trent.

CHASETOWN
This was a small gasworks in Cannock Chase which handled only 2,000 tons of coal a year from Yorkshire collieries, but the works had a private siding at Brownhills, on the Lichfield to Walsall line of the LNWR. Supplies would have arrived via Wichnor Junction and Lichfield.

COVENTRY
The gasworks were situated alongside the Coventry Canal at Exhall and served by the ex-LNWR Nuneaton to Coventry line over which the Midland Railway exercised running powers. It owned no railway wagons of its own and relied on those owned by collieries and the coal factors who contracted for its requirements. Annually its coal intake by contract was a little over 100,000 tons from Yorkshire, 40,000 tons from Derbyshire and 10,000 tons from North Staffordshire, plus regular purchases on the spot market. Most was purchased through national coal factors that specialised in gas coal, mainly the Birmingham firms of Lunt Bros. and Thomas Cash and Sons. The principal collieries were Nunnery near Sheffield, Thorncliffe and Barnsley Main, both near Barnsley.

DUDLEY and BRIERLEY HILL
Neither works were rail connected, coal for Dudley was unloaded at a dedicated siding at the LMS station at Dudley (one of three and assumed to be at Dudley High Level on the ex-LNWR South Staffordshire branch). Traffic for Brierley Hill was unloaded at the GWR station at Brettall Lane and carted by road to the gasworks. Records of coal consumption are incomplete but 40,000 tons a year is suggested, with supplies obtained from North Staffordshire (25%) and Derbyshire/Yorkshire (75%) with the most important suppliers being

the Birley Colliery near Sheffield and the Maltby Main colliery near Doncaster.

KIDDERMINSTER
In the late 1930s, Kidderminster purchased over 8,000 tons of gas coal a year, but this was recorded as being delivered to both Kidderminster and Bromsgrove. 1,500 tons came from North Staffordshire, 1,000 tons from North Wales and the balance from Yorkshire, the Elsecar and Hickleton collieries being the principal suppliers. One colliery that was not shown in the company records is Wath Main, although the colliery records show deliveries of 1,500 tons over this period. However, this is not important, as it could have been a spot purchase to cover a supply shortfall. The coal from north Wales would have been delivered direct to Kidderminster via the Great Western, the balance by the LMS to a Great Western connection, possibly Bordesley Sidings within Birmingham or via the ex-LNWR South Staffordshire line to Dudley.

LEAMINGTON PRIORS GAS CO.
By the late 1930s the works were using 20,000 tons a year, unloaded at a dedicated siding in the Great Western goods yard at Leamington Spa station. This arrived from north Wales (4,000 tons), north Staffordshire (2,000), Yorkshire (10,000) and the balance from Derbyshire. The most important source of supply was the Elsecar Colliery, near Barnsley on the former Great Central. There is ample evidence to show that some Leamington gas coal was routed via the Great Central and Banbury when the Great Central London Extension was opened, as freight accounts have survived. The Great Western would have delivered the coal from north Wales direct. This gas works owned a small fleet of thirty wagons.

LICHFIELD
A fairly small works with no direct rail connection, using 5,000 tons a year, obtained entirely from Yorkshire.

NUNEATON
The privately owned gas works used 10,000 tons a year, all from the Butterley Company pits in Derbyshire, the Company having a financial interest in the works.

REDDITCH
The gasworks had its own siding a short distance from Redditch station and received annually around 18,000 tons of coal, all of which came from Yorkshire with the Elsecar and Waleswood collieries the main suppliers. Both were on the LNER and coal would have been transferred to the LMS to work via Washwood Heath, Camp Hill, King's Norton and Barnt Green.

ROWLEY REGIS
Little is known about the gasworks consumption other than contracts totalling 2,000 tons with the Wath Main Colliery in Yorkshire and the Broughton and Plas Power Colliery in north Wales. A private siding serving this works was located on the GWR at Blowers Green.

SMETHWICK
This was another substantial gasworks using around 50,000 tons a year; it was located near Soho on the ex-LNWR, where there were private sidings serving the gasworks. Most supplies came from Yorkshire, with the Maltby and Yorkshire Main collieries being the principal source. Both collieries were on the LNER although the LMS also had access. The works purchased one hundred new railway wagons in the 1920s, built by the nearby Birmingham Railway Carriage and Wagon Company.

STOURPORT
A small gasworks using only 3,000 tons a year, almost all from Derbyshire or Yorkshire.

STOURBRIDGE
Using 30,000 tons a year, the Stourbridge gas works dealt mainly with Yorkshire and north Staffordshire collieries, but its few records are sketchy indeed. It also owned a small wagon fleet and was served by a private siding at Stourbridge Town on the Great Western.

TAMWORTH
Using only 8,000 tons a year, half of which came from the Apedale Colliery in north Staffordshire and the rest from Derbyshire and Yorkshire, Tamworth had coal sidings on both the ex-Midland and LNWR and coal would have been received at both.

TIPTON
Originally operated by the Tipton Urban District Council, the works were located near Tipton station on the former LNWR Stour valley line; their sidings were shared with the Mond Gas plant described later. Little is known of their consumption or source of their coal, except that a regular contract with the Wath Main Colliery in Yorkshire has been located in that company's records.

WALSALL
The gasworks were located on the ex-LNWR South Staffordshire branch at Pleck, where the Midland also had access. This was fortunate; almost all of the coal used came from collieries served by that railway. Consumption was around 50,000 tons a year, of which a third came from Low Moor Colliery at Kirkby, Notts, and the balance was spread between several other Notts and Derbyshire collieries. The Walsall gas works were municipally owned and operated their own fleet of fifty railway wagons.

Bescot Yard, the main marshalling yard of the former LNWR in the Birmingham area, showing in the foreground one of the former LNWR 0–8–2 tank engines. These powerful locomotives were used for shunting and short-distance trip workings and were able to work heavy trains of coal. The privately owned wagons give some indication of the extent of the distribution of the coal from the Cannock Chase collieries using the railway for distribution to Birmingham, the Black Country and all over southern England.

W. L. GOOD

WARWICK

The gasworks were located at Saltisford, on the western outskirts of the town and originally served by a basin on the Grand Union Canal and later by a siding off the main line of the Great Western Railway. An average of 12,000 tons a month was used. This came entirely from Yorkshire and Derbyshire, which would have been transported by the Midland and later the LMS to Bordesley Sidings in Birmingham where the Great Western would have taken over. The gasworks employed a small wagon fleet, supplemented by those of the contractors and collieries from where supplies were obtained.

WEST BROMWICH

The gasworks were located at Albion, a now-closed ex-LNWR station on the Birmingham to Wolverhampton line between Oldbury and Dudley Port. The coal came from Yorkshire and Derbyshire collieries and would have arrived via Toton, Wichnor Junction and Bescot. The works carbonised some 60,000 tons of coal a year, of which 10,000 tons came from north Staffordshire, the balance from Derbyshire and Yorkshire. The largest individual supplier was the Wath Main Colliery in Yorkshire, which supplied some 5,000 tons annually.

WILLENHALL

The gasworks were located near Short Heath on the Midland Railway Water Orton to Wolverhampton branch. Between twenty and twenty-five thousand tons a year were used, evenly divided between collieries in north Staffordshire, Yorkshire, north Wales and Derbyshire; it was largely purchased through local coal factors. The coal from Yorkshire and Derbyshire would have probably come via Water Orton and from north Staffordshire via Stone and Stafford. The Great Western, using a route via Shrewsbury and Wolverhampton, would haul the coal from north Wales.

WOLVERHAMPTON

Annual contracted requirements of 100,000 tons were purchased from north Staffordshire (12,000 tons) north Wales (5,000 tons), Derbyshire (6,000 tons), the rest came from Yorkshire, with the Birley Colliery near Sheffield the biggest supplier. The latter was on the former Great Central and transfer to the LMS was, from anecdotal evidence, carried out in the Nottingham area. The traffic was taken via Wichnor Junction and Walsall to Wolverhampton. The gasworks were located on the ex-LNWR between Wolverhampton and Bushbury and on the GWR near Stafford Road. Trade was, like most gasworks in this survey, carried on through local and national coal factors.

The LMS, until the early 1930s, appears to have delivered all coal originating on its network that travelled through Toton and Washwood Heath bound for Great Western destinations to Bordesley Sidings, even though there was a much shorter and more convenient route from Wichnor Junction, through Lichfield and Walsall and the South Staffordshire branch to reach the Great Western at Dudley. That the LMS preferred the Bordesley Junction route and the extra sixteen miles it traversed was the touch paper that ignited a substantial skirmish with one large coal consumer on the Great Western at Brierley Hill, who took on the LMS and won substantial freight concessions regardless of which route his Derbyshire and Yorkshire coal was forwarded, by enlisting the support of his suppliers under threat of transferring his coal business to south Wales collieries. On the other hand, it must be said that the facilities at Washwood Heath and Bordesley were designed to transfer large quantities of traffic on a daily basis and that the arrangements at Wichnor may not have been able to cope with this additional volume of coal traffic.

OTHER GASWORKS

There were other gasworks in the West Midlands for which no records survive. These include Solihull, Halesowen and Wednesbury. It was possible to pick up some transactions through the records of the Wath Main Colliery, a major supplier of gas coal all over the country, which recorded a contract with the Halesowen works in 1939 for 850 tons.

The manufacture of Mond Industrial Gas at Tipton and within the confines of the City of Birmingham works at Nechells provided another type of coal traffic. Mond Gas was suitable for industrial purposes only and could be made from any kind of coal. The plant at Tipton, operated by the South Staffordshire Mond Gas Co, owned its own coal wagons although much was delivered in colliery-owned wagons and even more by the adjoining canal. Suppliers included Holly Bank in Cannock Chase, Hamstead near Perry Barr on the outskirts of Birmingham, and Ansley Hall near Nuneaton.

It will be noted that all gasworks divided their coal purchases among several collieries, some dealing through colliery agents or coal factors and a lesser number dealing direct with the colliery. The reasons for this are simple: (1) many collieries mined gas coal only intermittently and gas coal was a small proportion of their output; this applies particularly to those in north Staffordshire. (2) Spreading business among several suppliers instilled a spirit of competition in both price and service, and (3) if an industrial dispute affected supplies from an individual colliery, there were always others to fill the gaps.

From the gas works point of view, by dealing with a coal factor, who had access to numerous collieries, the potential problems outlined under (3) were reduced. Birmingham was home to three very large factors who specialised in gas coal; these, and the extent of their trading, are described herein. Coal was normally supplied under annual contracts but shortfalls due to increased requirements or default of delivery were commonly rectified by transactions at the Birmingham Coal Exchange, where additional orders could be placed, often with collieries and merchants who were not regular contractors. Traffic of gas coal by rail continued into the early 1960s but the quantities decreased as natural North Sea gas replaced coal as a fuel. Conversion to North Sea gas started at Burton-on-Trent in 1959 and most of the gasworks in the Birmingham and Black Country areas had ceased working by the end of the 1960s.

ELECTRICITY

After gasworks, electric power generating stations were the second largest individual consumers of coal in the West Midlands. Coal used for electricity generation is totally different to that used for carbonising at gas works It is always small coal, ranging from slack (a very small coal bordering on dust), to what are known in the trade as nuts, pieces about the size of a walnut. It was almost always washed, and was mainly the broken leftovers after screening for larger pieces of coal for household or industrial use. Therefore, it was always the cheapest of coal and readily available from virtually any colliery in the country. Slack and small coal in particular was difficult to sell and often accumulated at the colliery. Therefore a generating station could take advantage of bargain parcels sold off by the colliery at the best price that could be obtained, simply to dispose of it.

The City of Birmingham Electric Supply Department, with major power stations at Nechells and Hams Hall, was the major supplier of electricity in the area. The company's Nechells works was alongside the gasworks of the same name and Hams Hall was between Water Orton and Arley on the Birmingham to Nuneaton line of the former Midland Railway. Few records of the Department exist, but fortunately a summary of coal contracts for 1933 has survived and was found among some documents that related to the Hamstead Colliery in the Staffordshire Records Office, unidentified and only confirmed by the signature on an otherwise anonymous copy of an accompanying letter.

BIRMINGHAM

In 1933 the two major power stations consumed 330,000 tons of coal that was obtained from collieries in Warwickshire, south Derbyshire, Leicestershire and Cannock Chase. Occasionally job lots were purchased from Nottinghamshire and north Derbyshire. As a detailed breakdown of the Gas Department's coal supplies was published in *Midland Record 20*, a similar dissection of a whole year's contracts for 1933 is detailed overleaf.

This picture shows a wagon with hopper doors discharging slack and small coal at a power station. In addition, we can see a considerable amount of detail on the body sill of the wagon, which was built by the Butterley Company in 1937. The label 'In Circuit Working' indicates that the vehicle was operated in block trains that ran between colliery and power station.

DERBYSHIRE RECORDS OFFICE

In addition, there were many references to spot purchases for quantities ranging up to 7,500 tons from the organisations above and several others from collieries as far away as south Yorkshire. Apologetically it was recorded that, 'we have at times resorted to buying coal on the spot market as the perennial shortage of railway wagons means that our suppliers cannot meet their commitments.' A further comment in this report is well worth reproducing here. The efficiency of the Department's railway wagon fleet is spotlighted in that each wagon took an average of eight days for a round trip to the supplying collieries, all of which were within a forty-mile radius of either Nechells or Hams Hall. By contrast, those of the Gas Department, which had to travel up to 150 miles for their coal supply, made only 25 journeys each year, an average of a little over 14 days per trip. A small flotilla of narrow boats was also owned, employed mainly in transporting coke dust from the various gas works within Birmingham to Nechells Power Station. The department itself owned 330 wagons, its fleet being founded in 1916 by the purchase of fifty wagons built by William Gittus of Penistone, Yorkshire, obtained secondhand from the Buxton Lime Firms Ltd..

One of the major coal contractors was the Samuel Barlow Coal Co. Ltd. which operated a small fleet of railway wagons in its own colours but will be eternally remembered, along with Fellows Morton and Clayton, for its fleet of narrow boats carrying coal on the entire canal network of the midlands and well beyond, particularly in the direction of London. Leonard Leigh of Walsall was another contractor who operated canal boats. Coal for the power station at Nechells could have been transported by canal, but it is considered that most of the contracts measured in boatloads were for a small power station at Summer Lane, in the heart of Birmingham, which had no rail connection and was, in 1933, in the throes of being phased out.

By the end of the 1930s, Birmingham Electric Supply Department was using 600,000 tons a year, Hams Hall taking the larger proportion. No records exist to show its origin, although it is possible that little was sent by canal, as Summer Lane was almost phased out by then. Coal received by the Nechells power station would have been routed via the Leicester to Burton-on-Trent line and then via Tamworth, whilst coal from Warwickshire could have been taken via Nuneaton and Water Orton, to the Tame and Rea Sidings situated close to the Washwood Heath marshalling yards. Coal obtained from collieries served by the ex-LNWR main line, may have been transferred at Nuneaton whilst coal for Hams Hall would have travelled from Kingsbury Station Junction via Whitacre Junction to the power station. [Later, in the 1950s, the editor recalls working on local trips taking coal from collieries on the Kingsbury branch to Hams Hall.]

CONTRACTOR	TONNAGE	COLLIERY OF ORIGIN
Samuel Barlow Coal Co.	4,000	Ansley Hall (Nuneaton)
	7,500	Minorca (Ashby de la Zouch)
	10,000	Pooley Hall (Tamworth)
	1,500	Shipley (Ilkeston, Derbyshire)
	300 boats	Holly Bank (Wolverhampton)
Mrs Amelia Brockhurst	5,200	Coleorton (Ashby de la Zouch)
	250 boats	Cannock Chase
Alexander Comley Ltd	450 boats	Baggeridge (Dudley)
	15,000	Brereton (Cannock Chase)
	27,500	Coventry
	30,000	Cadley Hill (South Derbyshire)
	12,500	Bretby (South Derbyshire)
	12,500	Kingsbury (Warwickshire)
T & M Dixon	5,200	Nuneaton
Haunchwood Colliery	10,000	Haunchwood (Nuneaton)
Frank Knight	100 boats	Cannock Chase
	6,000	Arley (Nuneaton)
	30,000	Birch Coppice (Tamworth)
Leamore Coal Co.	26,000	Baddesley (Warwickshire)
Leonard Leigh	20,000	Cannock and Rugeley
	15,000	Griff (Nuneaton)
	12,500	West Cannock (Cannock Chase)
Lunt Bros.	5,200	Exhall (Nuneaton)
	11,500	Newdigate (Nuneaton)
Moira Colliery	15,000	Rawdon (Ashby de la Zouch)
Pooley Hall Colliery	20,000	Pooley Hall (Tamworth)
Spencer Abbot and Co.	300 boats	Aldridge (Walsall)
D. W. Stephenson Ltd	12,500	Whitwick (South Leicestershire)
	6,500	Binley (Coventry)
Wilson Carter and Pearson	5,000	Tamworth

A typical 20-ton steel body coal wagon of the type that was slowly introduced to replace the traditional open wagon of 10- and 12-ton capacity. This example was allocated to the generating station at Ironbridge and, apart from the small lettering at bottom right, was identical to those operated by the Wolverhampton works as described in the article.

COLLECTION PHIL COUTANCHE

WEST MIDLANDS JOINT ELECTRICITY AUTHORITY, WOLVERHAMPTON

This was an electric supply authority based at the Wolverhampton Corporation's Walsall Street power station and formed in the 1920s to assume control of the former corporation-owned power station and to provide electricity over a wide area of south Staffordshire and the Black Country. As a corporate body, it also incorporated the former Walsall Corporation's power station at Birchills, opened in 1916, which also used canal transport exclusively until a railway connection was made in 1949. There was also the Ocker Hill power station at Wednesbury, which also relied on canal transport until 1943.

Although most of the coal used at Wolverhampton was delivered by canal, it was well known as the owner of a fleet of 20-ton steel coal wagons, probably inspired by the Great Western Railway who offered a favourable carriage rate to those companies that transported their raw materials in such vehicles. A small trial order was placed with the wagon builders Charles Roberts of Wakefield, then a more substantial purchase of 150 similar wagons was made from the Metro-Cammell works at Washwood Heath.

There are few known extant records of this company, or for that matter any other electricity generating companies, either privately or municipally owned, but it is considered that it was of similar size to its Birmingham counterpart and consumed around 300,000 tons of coal in the early 1930s. Its geographic location would suggest that this was obtained from the Cannock Chase and north Staffordshire coalfields, but the only known sources are those that were delivered by rail, 13,000 tons a year by rail from the Highley Colliery on the Severn Valley Railway. It is possible that this authority was using overall some half a million tons of coal a year by the end of the 1930s.

Electric power for Coventry was generated by a new power station at Longford, built in 1926, beside the Oxford Canal but also served by a siding off the former Wyken Colliery branch of the LMS. The only surviving records show that almost all coal consumed was delivered by canal, mostly from such nearby collieries as Exhall, Coventry, Griff and Newdigate.

Coal supplies to the power stations at Birchills, near Walsall, and Ockers Hill, West Bromwich, have already been described as being delivered by canal until at least the middle of the Second World War, and subsequent deliveries by rail would have been under government control, therefore its origin cannot be determined, but under the regulations in force at the time, if the coal was suitable, it was to be obtained from the nearest colliery; in this instance it would be from Cannock Chase.

WATERWORKS AND OTHER MUNICIPAL CONSUMERS

The third group of consumers of coal under the category of public utilities or services, are the various instrumentalities that are part of an overall municipal council which is responsible for, in a large city like Birmingham, education, police, hospitals, swimming baths, parks and gardens, road works and law enforcement. Invariably their coal purchases were through local coal merchants or smaller coal factors and the coal was delivered by road from the nearest railway sidings, or, in the case of Birmingham and the Black Country, often by canal.

A Committee made up from representatives of the various departments usually carried out coal purchases. The City of Birmingham General Purposes Coal Sub-Sub Committee (subsequently referred to in an abbreviated form) was responsible for the annual purchase of 100,000 tons of coal, divided into over a hundred individual contracts, supplying, with the exception of Gas and Electricity, every department in the city. A representative of the

coal purchasing committee of the Gas Department was also a member and offered expert advice in instances where unsatisfactory coal or service had been experienced, and provided access to the Gas Department's coal testing plant at Saltley. In particular, the Brereton Colliery near Rugeley was frequently singled out for poor quality and as a result lost several contracts. It should not be considered that Brereton coal was sub-standard; other departments also used the same coal successfully. One of the purposes of the Coal Buying Committee was to ensure that each department received the most suitable coal at the best available price.

By the end of 1939 the Gas Department was purchasing, for all purposes, some one-and-a-half million tons a year, and the Electricity Department 600,000 tons. If we add the quantity purchased by the Coal Purchasing Committee, then we find that the City of Birmingham was consuming about two and a quarter million tons of coal every year. From 1916 the Electricity Department coal purchases were made by the Gas Department, a situation that continued until 1933, when the Electricity Department became responsible for its own contracts. In 1934 the coal purchases of all other bodies within the City of Birmingham were centralised by one committee, into which the Water Department and Sewage authority reluctantly agreed to join at a later date, having previously considered that their existing arrangements were satisfactory and should be immune to interference. It will become apparent that each individual location had its own preference for the type of coal supplied, and this was generally continued: there was no standardisation of boilers or furnaces and the wide variety of appliances in use were, after trial and error, supplied with the type of fuel that experience had shown was the best for their purpose.

Over a hundred separate contracts had to be negotiated with several contractors and factors, for deliveries which ranged from over 8,000 tons a year to just a couple of lorry loads. An example is the Health Department, responsible for hospitals, nursing homes, convalescent homes and a laundry. A separate contract was raised for eighteen different locations for this department alone. The various pumping stations of the Water Department used 12,000 tons a year. Pumping stations at Edgbaston, Frankley, Aston, Whitacre, Perry Well, Shortheath Well and Longbridge were located in the Birmingham area, and as none were located beside a canal, it is assumed that coal was delivered by rail to the nearest sidings, although Whitacre had its own sidings. At least their forty-plus boilers were standardised and one coal was suitable throughout.

This was a specific steam coal from the Baddesley Colliery near Atherstone and the contractor was Evesons (Coals) Ltd. In addition, Evesons were also responsible for deliveries to Bewdley, Bucknell, Cleobury Mortimer, Cleobury Town, Hagley, Knighton, Ludlow, Pen-y-bont, Rhayader and Northfields, delivering Best Hard Steam Coal from the Cannock Chase Colliery at Hednesford to these locations.

It is most fortunate that the records of the City of Birmingham Coal Buying Committee have been preserved and were recently made available at the Birmingham Central Library. Detailed below are the remainder of the contracts for the year 1st April 1938 to 31st March 1939. Rather than divide each department into individual delivery points, the Departmental total is shown, separated into department, contractor, colliery of origin and tonnage delivered.

BATHS DEPARTMENT		
T. Mottershead and Co.	Brownhills (Cannock Chase)	6,330
Evesons (Coals) Ltd.	Baddesley (Warwickshire)	1,325
	Birch Coppice (Tamworth)	775
EDUCATION DEPARTMENT		
Selly Oak Coal and Coke Co.	Binley (Coventry)	1,500
C. P. Perry and Sons	Griff (Nuneaton)	1,500
Frank Knight Ltd.	Desford (Leicestershire)	1,000
Evesons (Coals) Ltd.	Snibston (Leicestershire)	1,000
ESTATES DEPARTMENT		
T. Mottershead and Co.	Brownhills (Cannock Chase)	30
HEALTH DEPARTMENT		
Alexander Comley Limited	Haunchwood (Nuneaton)	6,000
	Kingsbury (Warwickshire)	6,650
	West Cannock (Cannock Chase)	2,850
Frank Knight Ltd.	Arley (Nuneaton)	1,000
	Birch Coppice (Tamworth)	380
	East Cannock (Cannock Chase)	40
	Pontyberem (S. Wales, anthracite)	10
T. Mottershead and Co.	Mid Cannock (Cannock Chase)	8,300
	Brownhills (Cannock Chase)	1,300
C. P. Perry and Sons	West Cannock (Cannock Chase)	105
	Birch Coppice (Tamworth)	45
	Pontyberem (S. Wales, anthracite)	61
	New Dynant (S.Wales, anthracite)	27
	East Cannock (Cannock Chase)	15
J. C. Abbott and Co. Ltd.	Whitwick (Leicestershire)	272
	Kingsbury (Warwickshire)	35
	Birch Coppice (Tamworth) bagged	260

Evesons (Coals) Ltd.	Cannock and Rugeley (Cannock Chase)	850
Spencer Abbott and Co.	Birch Coppice (Tamworth)	110
T. Foster and Sons	Graigola (S. Wales)	7

MARKETS AND FAIRS DEPARTMENT
(mostly for meat market)

Frank Knight Ltd.	Cannock and Rugeley (Cannock Chase)	10
	Brereton (Cannock Chase)	1,550
	Cannock Chase	35

MENTAL DEFICIENCY ACT COMMITTEE

Frank Knight Ltd.	Brereton (Cannock Chase)	850
Evesons (Coals) Ltd.	Cannock and Rugeley (Cannock Chase)	870
	Arley (Nuneaton)	500
Spencer Abbott Ltd.	Brereton (Cannock Chase)	430
Wood and Co.	Kingsbury (Warwickshire)	1,270

MENTAL HOSPITALS COMMITTEE

South Staffs Coal Agency	Sandwell Park (Birmingham) by canal	4,100
Frank Knight Ltd.	Coventry (Coventry)	105
	Cannock Chase	20
Evesons (Coals) Ltd.	Kingsbury (Warwickshire)	3,000
C. P. Perry and Sons	Pooley Hall (Tamworth)	4,300

PARKS AND GARDENS COMMITTEE

T. Mottershead and Co.	Brownhills (Cannock Chase)	235
	West Cannock (Cannock Chase)	10
	Ammanford (S. Wales, anthracite)	20

PUBLIC ASSISTANCE COMMITTEE

T. Mottershead and Co.	Cannock and Rugeley (Cannock Chase)	3,000
	Conduit (Cannock Chase)	2,000
	Brownhills (Cannock Chase) by canal	1,500
J. C. Abbott and Co.	Birch Coppice (Tamworth)	450
Frank Knight Ltd.	Brereton (Cannock Chase)	3,400
	Cannock and Rugeley (Cannock Chase)	26
	Pontyberem (S. Wales, anthracite)	326
Alexander Comley Ltd.	Cannock Chase	2,500
South Staffs Coal Agency	Hamstead (Birmingham)	500
C. P. Perry and Son	Birch Coppice (Tamworth)	680
	West Cannock (Cannock Chase)	50
	Holly Bank (Wolverhampton)	25
	Snibston (Leicestershire)	20

PUBLIC WORKS DEPARTMENT

Lawrence Miller Ltd.	Arley (Nuneaton)	400
	West Cannock (Cannock Chase)	415
	Cannock and Rugeley (Cannock Chase)	20
	Ocean Merthyr (S. Wales)	150
Spencer Abbott and Co.	Pooley Hall (Tamworth)	100
T. Mottershead and Co.	Brownhills (Cannock Chase)	1,400

TRANSPORT DEPARTMENT

| Frank Knight Ltd. | Birch Coppice (Tamworth) | 150 |

WATCH COMMITTEE
This consisted of law courts, police stations and prisons.

J. C. Abbott and Co. Ltd	Whitwick (Leicestershire)	210
Alexander Comley	Bretby (South Derbyshire)	340
C. P. Perry and Sons	Bretby (South Derbyshire)	600
Lawrence Miller Ltd.	Haunchwood (Nuneaton)	300

It will be noticed that the biggest coal factor in Birmingham, Wilson, Carter and Pearson, is totally absent from this listing and the very large firm of J. C. Abbott is only represented in a minor way. Their absence, for whatever reason, enabled some relatively smaller coal factors, with local depots, such as Thomas Mottershead and Co. of Soho Pool; C. P. Perry and Son of Camp Hill, Lawley Street and King's Heath; Lawrence Miller of Curzon Street, Lawley Street, Tyseley, Acocks Green, Monument Lane, Soho Pool, Camp Hill and Erdington; The Selly Oak Coal and Coke Co. and Frank Knight of Chester Street and Lawley Street, to supply the various City of Birmingham departments.

A close watch was maintained on quality, and any deficiency quickly pointed out to the contractor who ensured that representatives from the supplying colliery participated in any arbitration that followed. The records also show that the large contractor, Spencer Abbott and Co, anxious to maintain supplies when the contracted colliery could not keep up with its orders, surreptitiously substituted a similar coal of the same grade, but this was found out immediately; this is not an isolated case, other municipalities and consumers have reported similar cases of substitution.

The London Midland and Scottish Railway was the main beneficiary of this business, every supplying colliery was located on its system and, with the exception of some deliveries made by canal, would have handled it exclusively. The only other exception would have been the few wagons from south Wales where, the most likely route would have been by the Great Western to the Birmingham area, but it is possible that the anthracite may have arrived via the ex-LNWR route from south Wales.

Comparison with the more detailed contracts for 1934–5 show that several local collieries were no longer patronised; these include Tamworth Colliery at Tamworth, Aldridge at Walsall (which had closed), and Cadley Hill in south Derbyshire. Contractors deleted included Lunt Bros, Fox and Perry and Round and Downs. Another contractor was Wood and Co, vaguely referred to in the minutes, but possibly the well-known contractor with the colourful yellow wagons that was based in London; there was no coal factor named Wood in the greater Birmingham area. The 1938/9 contracts were restricted by the Coal Selling Scheme which restricted supplies and, in the words of the Buying Committee, 'tell us what coal we can buy and damn our rights to buy what is most suitable for us at the best price'. This in turn resulted in only one quote being received for several contracts, pushing up prices and stifling competition. Coal was also purchased on the spot market, and some was delivered by road. An extreme case of the latter is a contract of Spencer Abbott and Co for 8,750 tons ex-Brownhills Colliery in Cannock Chase to the swimming baths, this contract of 1934/5 replaced one shared by Brownhills and the Hamstead Colliery near Great Barr in Birmingham.

The only other known contract for a public utility in the whole district is one for the Wolverhampton waterworks, for 7,000 tons from the Highley Colliery in Shropshire and delivered direct by the Great Western Railway. There were further sewage works around Birmingham and each of the local municipal governing bodies would have its own purchasing arrangements, but, as far as I am aware, no details of any have survived. A surviving record of transactions covered by the Warwickshire County Council covers only part of that county for the late 1930s, the volume of coal involved was less than seven thousand tons, which required a committee of five to administer it. Finally, one of the very surprising features of this operation is that no purchases of coke, which was in considerable use, were recorded. *To be continued.*

Looking east from Fenchurch Street on 19th April 1959. The curvature of the line here necessitated a permanent speed restriction of 15 mph which was not always strictly adhered to by the late-running trains. On the left of the photograph is a train waiting to depart, headed by engine 80073, whilst just visible is a train approaching the station. This was the ex 12.10 p.m. from Shoeburyness headed by Engine 42500 running bunker first. To its right, standing light, Engine No. 80033 may have been waiting to back up onto the incoming stock in readiness to work a passenger train out of the terminus.
H. B. PRIESTLEY

Leaving Fenchurch Street station on 21st June 1958 is a 3-cylinder engine No. 42512 at the head of a stopping passenger train. Running chimney first was the preferred way of most enginemen in working trains out of Fenchurch Street. As there were no turntables available, bunker-first running was unavoidable in one direction. The arched overall roof, which spanned the platforms at its terminal end, is visible in the background.   H. B. PRIESTLEY

Experiences of an Engineman on the LT & SR During the Last Years of Steam

by JIM JACKSON

DURING 1959 the overhead line electrification of the LT & SR east of Gas Factory Junction was well underway. As this was mostly at 25kV A/C it was necessary to convert the existing section of electrified line between Fenchurch Street and the Gas Factory Junction from 1500V D/C to conform to the new system. As well as being electrified, the line was also re-signalled with new colour light signals controlled from fewer signal boxes, some of them newly built but covering a much larger area. To service the electrification and re-signalling schemes, a number of engineering trains were constantly required and it had been decided that Tilbury Depot would provide the necessary power to work these trains. This meant that additional footplate staff were needed.

In 1959 I was a fireman in lodging accommodation at Doncaster and, as Tilbury had by then been included in the Eastern Region promotional area, I decided to apply for one of the vacancies being advertised. Somewhat to my surprise, at the second attempt in early 1960, my name appeared on the successful applicants' list. As I was only a fireman at Doncaster, I first had to appear before Inspector Mitchell to complete the examination to become a driver and, having passed, received my one-way free pass from Doncaster to Tilbury on Monday 22nd February 1960. I was then aged 26 years and a driver, having bypassed the intermediate stage of passed fireman or, as it was alternatively known, spare driver. At that time I was one of the youngest, if not the youngest, regular driver (as opposed to a passed fireman) on the whole of the Eastern Region of British Railways. Here, I must stress that this was not due to any superior ability on my part. Promotion was strictly on a seniority basis and, as a comparatively large number of driving vacancies had been declared at Tilbury, the depot was attracting staff from other depots within the promotional area. I was not moving into entirely unknown territory as before moving to Doncaster I had been a fireman at Newark, from

where four men had moved to Tilbury a year or two prior to Newark's closure in January 1959. I had visited one of them, Douglas (Jock) Thompson, who gave me details of the depot's link structure including the type of work I could expect to be on. There were four main links at Tilbury which were:

Link 1   Passenger
Link 2   Goods
Link 3   Spare
Link 4   Shunting

Under normal circumstances, I would have been placed in the bottom link at the depot, which was the shunting link, but Jock Thompson informed me that as this link was completely filled by senior drivers who did not want main line work, I would be placed in the Spare link. This link covered not only the wiring and engineers trains but also temporary vacancies in the other three links, which included working outer suburban passenger trains on the whole of the LT&S system of lines. In the event, I spent about half of my time working passenger trains – this was a schoolboy's dream come true! Shunting work at Tilbury consisted of manning the diesel shunting locomotives at Tilbury, Grays and Purfleet but not the locomotives on Tilbury Docks, as these came within the jurisdiction of the Port of London Authority.

Footplate staff were allowed just one day to move to their new depot and to find lodging accommodation and, on the very next day, it was down to the tedious task of road (or route) learning. Fortunately, I was not on my own as a passed fireman from Hornsey depot, Charlie Brown, had also moved on the same promotional list for a driving position at Tilbury. I had known Charlie from early on in his railway career, which had commenced at Sleaford, a town not all that far from Newark. Our colleagues at Tilbury, who were Cockneys rather than Essex men, having the Cockney sense of humour and their easygoing way of life, quickly accepted us. We therefore made route-learning trips on engines manned by

Tilbury men whenever possible. All in all we had about fourteen weeks road learning. This may seem a long time but it must be borne in mind that in order to run trains to a four-minute headway during the morning and evening peak periods, the line was very intensively signalled. The signalling included a large number of Intermediate Block Signals, which, at that time were not specially identified, and as special instructions applied to them, it was essential to know their exact location. The special instructions in the Sectional Appendix ran to two pages of closely spaced print, the first line of which read – 'The object of intermediate block signals is to allow a train to leave the signal box in rear before the preceding train has passed the signal box in advance …'. This, in a nutshell, describes their purpose.

We had been road-learning for several weeks when we had the misfortune to encounter a rather unpleasant incident. On the day in question, we travelled on an Austerity 2–8–0 light engine to Pitsea, from where it reversed towards Barking to pick up an engineers train en-route. Shortly after leaving Pitsea, we were stopped and informed that there had been an accident on the down line in which a Permanent Way Inspector had been hit by a passenger train and fatally injured. We were allowed to proceed at caution after being advised to keep a sharp lookout. Sure enough, further along the line, we came across the stationary passenger train and just beyond it the body of the unfortunate man that had been moved clear of running lines. We continued our route-learning, eventually arriving at Fenchurch Street station where we entered the cab of an engine about to work a train to Tilbury; the driver was Gerry Harper. I started to tell him about the fatality when I suddenly stopped as Gerry was looking at me in rather a strange way. After a pause, he then said very quietly, "I know, I was the driver". We were later informed that it was not the first accident in which poor Gerry had recently been involved. Today, when a driver is involved in a similar incident, he is relieved as soon as possible and

No. 42220 entering Barking station on 7th March 1959 at the head of the Saturdays Only 2.10 p.m. Fenchurch Street – Thorpe Bay stopping passenger train. Rebuilding and remodelling the station was well underway but there is little evidence yet of the installation of the overhead line electrification. H. B. PRIESTLEY

Tilbury Town station, looking towards Fenchurch Street on 21st June 1958. LMS Class 4F No. 44228 is seen running through the station on its journey to Tilbury Riverside station at the head of a Swedish Lloyd Line boat train. Tilbury enginemen were involved in working these trains as a limited number of drivers signed the route through to St. Pancras, the boat trains starting and terminating point.
                    H. B. PRIESTLEY

Tilbury Riverside station, again taken on 21st June 1958, with Engine 80101 entering at the head of a train. Part of the carriage sidings can be seen on the right. Besides the LT&S services, the station was also the destination for boat trains connecting with the ocean-going liners. Porters very much welcomed these trains as they usually received a generous tip for transferring passengers' heavy luggage between train and boat and vice-versa.

H. B. PRIESTLEY

booked off duty, with pay, for several days. Not so in the 1960s, when a driver was expected to work on as if nothing had happened.

At this point, I should also mention a far more serious accident that had involved Tilbury Depot some two years earlier. On 30th January 1958, passed fireman Reginald Barnes of Tilbury Depot was in charge of engine 80079 and working the 6.35 p.m. train from Fenchurch Street to Shoeburyness. Besides the darkness, the evening was in the grip of a thick London fog in which visibility was down to an estimated 10 yards. In the vicinity of Dagenham East, Barnes ran into the rear of the preceding train that was just starting to move away after having been brought to a stand by adverse signals. As usual at this time of the evening, both trains were heavily loaded and, unfortunately, 10 people met their deaths besides another 89 who were injured in the collision, although neither Barnes nor his fireman were seriously hurt.

The enquiry into the accident was somewhat involved, but the conclusion was eventually reached that, in the thick fog, Barnes had mistaken his whereabouts and had passed the signal protecting the occupied section, Upney's starter, at 'danger'. Reg Barnes always maintained that the signal he had passed was in the

'clear' position, this causing doubt in the minds of some Tilbury drivers as to the exact cause of the crash. When I arrived at Tilbury, Reg Barnes, by then a driver, was confined to shed duties but later on he was allowed to resume driving trains on the main line. His fireman on the occasion of the accident was Steve Fryer, a competent and knowledgeable railwayman who later progressed into management grades. Generally speaking, Steve would not comment on the accident, but he did once tell me that he thought himself lucky to be alive as the solebar of the rear coach passed underneath his cab seat.

Our road-learning was almost over; the final short stretch of line to cover was the freight-only single line Thames Haven branch. This was easy enough but it was here that we encountered an unusual operating practice. For heavy trains coming off the single line at Thames Haven Junction, the gradient coupled with the curvature of the line presented a problem. To enable trains to have a run at the gradient, drivers of heavy freight trains were instructed to bring their trains to a stand at the Up Branch distant signal when it was at 'caution' and not to proceed until it was taken off.

On 30th April 1960, with my road-learning completed, I finally signed my route card – at least I had the long days of

clear weather in front of me. The route card was, and is, an important document in which a driver acknowledged that he had a thorough understanding of the roads, permanent speed restrictions, gradients, etc, applicable to all lines in both directions over which he was going to work. This prevented him, in the event of an accident or mishap, from putting forward the excuse that he was unaware of his whereabouts. It was forbidden for a driver to work over a section of line for which he did not sign the route. Locomotives used on passenger trains from within the system were all of the 2–6–4T wheel arrangement. There were two main types, the LMS 3-cylinder engines, which had been especially designed with the LT&S in mind and the BR Standard 80,000 Class. On occasions we also encountered the later LMS/BR Fairburn 2-cylinder engines. As Plaistow Shed was by then virtually closed and was only used for stabling engines, particularly in between the two peak periods, the 2–6–4Ts were allocated between the depots of Shoeburyness and Tilbury.

Shoeburyness had the 3-cylinder engines whilst Tilbury had the BR Standards, although there was a certain amount of interchangeability. I came to prefer the 2-cylinder types, but Shoeburyness men preferred their own 3-

cylinder engines which certainly rode very well; it probably all came down to regular usage. Under normal circumstances engines would work between Shoeburyness and Fenchurch Street on a full tank of water but, if a delay occurred, there could be problems, so before a run, I always took the precaution of filling the boiler as full as possible when topping up the tanks. This was a piece of good advice drummed into me by Phil Timms, my regular driver when I was a young fireman at the small Nottinghamshire depot of Southwell. As the passenger service was geared to the morning and evening peak periods, it was possible to allocate one engine to two crews. I can only remember that 80073 was allocated to my friend Jock Thompson on one shift and to Ray Shoebridge on the other. To encourage crews to take a pride in their regular engine there was available an issue of 'Derby Paste' which was used to polish up the brass and copper fittings in the cab. Derby Paste, I believe, had originated on the Midland Railway, hence its name.

Coaching stock consisted mainly of 8- and 11-coach sets. The 8-coach sets were employed on all parts of the system but the 11-coach sets were usually confined to the direct route via Upminster. Diesel Multiple Units worked the Upminster – Ockendon – Grays service and, as this was covered by Tilbury, I eventually had to be trained on DMUs. I had been working trains for less than a fortnight when, to my great consternation, on Friday 13th May 1960, I was rostered to work the second half of the Line Manager's Special Train carrying out an inspection of the line. In addition to the Line Traffic Manager, Mr J. W. Dedman and his senior staff, the special also conveyed members of the Basildon Development Corporation that included Lt. Gen. Sir Humphrey Gale, Sir John Macpherson and Mr R. C. C. Boniface. My fireman was H. Pumfrett and, after booking on duty at 12.20 p.m., we walked to Tilbury East Junction where we relieved Tilbury men on engine 80136 at 12.55 p.m. To my relief, accompanying us on the footplate was our local footplate inspector who had an extensive knowledge of the LT & SR system. He must have known of my circumstances as he proved to be most helpful in pointing out to me some of the more obscure locations at which I had to stop.

Before we left Tilbury at 1.40 p.m., the party dined, and, as this was before the clampdown on the drinking of alcohol on

duty, perhaps also wined. Our load was only two vehicles which was fortunate as the special working involved a certain amount of propelling. When we had nearly completed our tour of inspection, our inspector asked me if I would allow one of the titled gentlemen (I forget which one) to drive the engine back to Fenchurch Street – I could hardly refuse! The good gentleman occupied the driving seat, setting off at a fast pace. I was given to understand that he had had experience of driving engines before, but I soon formed the opinion that this was very little. He was giving the engine a good thumping and I began to fear that there was a possibility of us hitting the buffer stops at Fenchurch Street, but my fears were unfounded as, after passing Gas Factory Junction, our inspector tactfully suggested that I should take over for the remainder of the journey into the terminus. He vacated the driving seat with an expression on his face that clearly stated, "There we are, that's the way to do it!" On arrival at Fenchurch Street, the whole party left the train, all smiles and thanks. They had had a pleasant day out. So had I! All that remained to be done was to take the stock empty to Stratford (East London) for which I was provided with a pilotman over the stretch of line that I did not sign and then return light engine to Tilbury.

In the spring of that year (1960) the shortage of firemen on the LT&S became acute and to help alleviate matters, a recruitment drive took place in selected parts of the country in which there was a degree of unemployment. At Shoeburyness, this even involved taking on University students during their summer holidays. As some of the men recruited for Tilbury were not of the best material, it was often necessary for drivers to give these men some form of practical assistance. As part of the deal and, as an incentive to move, they were paid a generous weekly lodging allowance, which often meant that their take-home pay was greater than that of their drivers. This caused an understandable amount of resentment. Fortunately for all concerned, the 2-6-4T would respond to indifferent firing helped by the fact that the best quality steam coal was provided at both Tilbury and Shoeburyness depots.

Passenger work at Tilbury was arguably the most interesting, a day's work was covered by what was known as a diagram, each being given its own identification number. One that I worked on many

occasions was Tilbury No. 4, a diagram that many men disliked, as the booking-on time was 2.30 in the morning. After preparing the engine for its day's work, for which we were allowed one hour, we ran light engine bunker-first to Fenchurch Street Station where we coupled onto a short train of coaching stock in readiness to work the 5.10 am. to Shoeburyness. Our arrival at Fenchurch Street was some time before the train was due away as, in cold weather, it was necessary to steam-heat the stock. With the limited number of coaches behind the bunker, this was not a hard train to work. On reaching our destination at Shoeburyness, we detached our coaches and dropped onto the engine shed where we cleaned the fire, turned, coaled and fully watered the engine in readiness for working back to Fenchurch Street. My diaries show this to be the 8.16 a.m. loaded to eleven coaches but, as I do not have the details of this particular train, I shall describe working the eleven-car sets from a general point of view.

Before departing, our guard would walk up to the engine to advise us of our load and where we were booked to stop. The guards assessed the train at 313 tons tare but what it finally weighed when fully loaded with commuters is anybody's guess. Trains worked by Tilbury crews were limited to where they stopped, many stations en route being run through at speed. When once well underway I usually worked the engine on full regulator and 15% cut-off, but from Pitsea, at the start of the 4½ mile climb up Laindon bank, it was necessary to drop the cut-off down. The initial gradient on leaving Pitsea was 1 in 110 and for trains calling there it needed quite an effort to get underway again. Matters were not helped by the fact that the station was on a curve, which meant that station staff had to relay the guard's right-away signal. Once over the top at Laindon, I would notch up to 15% cut-off, in which position, with a full head of steam, the eighty thousands would comfortably time a train. Most trains stopped at Barking where there was a surface interchange with trains of the London underground system and it was here that a number of passengers alighted. From Barking there was not much scope for high-speed running as there were severe speed restrictions over the curve between Gas Factory Junction and Campbell Road Junction and again through Stepney Station. The final 1¼ miles from Stepney into Fenchurch Street did not require

Tilbury Shed Yard and area, taken on 21st June 1958, with, to the left, the main running lines from Tilbury Riverside to Fenchurch Street. The coaling plant features in the centre whilst just visible behind the prominent signal post is a diesel mechanical shunting locomotive, which may have been used as the Tilbury Riverside station shunter employed mainly in the movement of coach stock. Engine No. 41981, just to the left of the diesel locomotive, was an 0–6–2 Tank engine of LT&S origin. Two BR Standard 2–6–4 Tank engines are visible, in the centre is 80080 and on the extreme left standing on the buffer stops we can also see 80087.
                                                                                                          H. B. PRIESTLEY

Five 4–4–2 Tank engines Nos. 41945, 41941, 41928, 41946 and 41939 stored outside Tilbury engine shed on 15th March 1958. The writer would dearly like to have handled one of these, but by the time he had arrived at Tilbury they had all gone. By all accounts, they were capable engines on the LT&S system, but when displaced and moved away to other areas they were not always liked. In the East Midlands they gained the nickname 'Crooners'.
                                                                                                          H. B. PRIESTLEY

much effort; hopefully, the fireman would have run his fire down in order not to emit steam from the safety valves or smoke from the chimney.

Throughout the journey a degree of skill was needed in order to bring the train to a stand in the correct position at the platforms. Coaches normally in use on the LT&S were equipped with the automatic vacuum brake. Before a train could move away, in order to release the brakes, a vacuum had to be created along the whole length of the train pipe by the ejectors on the engine. To apply the brakes, the driver had to admit air into the system via the brake handle in his cab. This air had to travel the whole length of the train pipe, which meant that it was often many seconds, depending upon the length of the train, before anything happened and the brakes started to bite. The same applied when releasing, as, when the brake handle was returned to the off position, it took the ejectors some time to eject all the air and fully release the brakes. To effect a smooth and gentle stop, it was necessary for the brakes to be slowly coming off. This technique was known to enginemen as 'stopping on a rising brake'. It was a source of satisfaction to bring a train gently to a stand within the coaching limits of a platform. On arrival at Fenchurch Street Station, as far as Tilbury No. 4 diagram was concerned, our day's work was nearly over. After the coaching stock had been removed, we ran light engine to Plaistow Engine shed from where we travelled home passenger.

One of the easiest diagrams to work was Tilbury No. 6, for which we booked on duty at 3.55 p.m. and travelled passenger to Shoeburyness. On arrival there, we obtained our engine and, after preparation duties, worked the 7.02 p.m. to Tilbury from where we worked a parcels train to Woodgrange Park, eventually returning Light Engine to Tilbury Depot to book off duty. Before returning from Woodgrange Park, we made time to have a cup of tea and something to eat which was usually fish and chips purchased from a shop conveniently situated just outside the station. With a decent mate, this could be a pleasant day out.

Life at Tilbury was not without its little incidents. When booking off duty one afternoon, I was met by our local footplate inspector who informed me that my fireman on the next day's working to Fenchurch Street was to be Fred Whitehouse. It transpired that Fred was

the one-millionth premium bond winner and although his win was not one of the larger prizes, the premium bond people wished to make the maximum amount of publicity from Fred's win. It was therefore arranged for television cameras and the press to meet our train on its arrival at Fenchurch Street. To give the occasion a little more glamour, our inspector asked me if I would allow Fred to drive the train into the terminus. As I did not particularly wish to be media fodder, I readily agreed to his request; in any case, as Fred was a passed fireman we would have split the day's firing and driving between the two of us. After arrival at Fenchurch Street there was the usual handshakes and congratulatory remarks, during which Fred was presented with a basket of fruit. I kept well out of the way!

Before leaving the subject of passenger trains, there was one escapade from which I was lucky to emerge unscathed. While working an early afternoon train out of Fenchurch Street, together with my fireman, we went into the first compartment of the coach next to the engine to enjoy a cup of tea, forgetting that we had left the injector working (the injector is the device which forces water into the boiler). By the time we had realised our mistake, the boiler was, to use a common phrase 'full up to the whistle'. There were two big problems with an overfull boiler, the first and most serious being that water instead of steam would enter the cylinders when the regulator was opened; the second was that water would enter the vacuum ejector, preventing it from functioning properly and so cause a brake application.

On receiving the right-away signal from the guard, with the cylinder cocks open, I slightly cracked open the regulator and, working on as fine a cut-off as possible, we slowly moved out of the platform. Fortunately, my fireman was an experienced Tilbury man who managed to keep the fire as hot as possible without allowing the engine to blow off at the safety valves. This did the trick as it allowed most of the water to dry out in the superheater and, although we lost time, we managed to keep going to our first stop at Barking, some 7½ miles down the line. Here the boiler gauge glass showed that the water was just one inch from the top. We had had a very lucky escape!

I did very little driving on freight trains as I did not sign the route over which most of these trains ran, but I did a considerable amount of work on engineers

trains in connection with the electrification programme. These trains fell into a number of categories, running under the various headings of foundation, auger, cement, steel, wiring and pantograph, each one allocated to a different type of work. Motive power provided for these trains was either a 2–6–4T or an Austerity 2–8–0.

One interesting working, although it could hardly be described as a train, took place in the summer of 1961. The firm of May and Baker had extensive works with siding accommodation on the north side of the line, in the vicinity of Dagenham on the main line via Upminster. During that summer, while the firm's boilers were under repair, they hired a locomotive, changed weekly, from British Railways, to act as a temporary boiler replacement. May and Baker's sidings were reached from an 'in section' ground frame located on the down line and it was here that a problem arose. This frame could not be worked unless a vehicle standing on its approach side completed an electrical circuit. The engine for M & B was at first dragged dead on its own and, to overcome the problem, the ever-resourceful Cockneys placed a clinker shovel across the two rails, which completed the electrical circuit. This unauthorised method of working the frame must have come to the notice of the authorities as an instruction was issued to the effect that, when it was necessary to change the engine, a brake van must be placed behind the dead engine and left on the running line. From my diaries I note that one of the engines loaned to M & B was engine 42521, this being placed in their sidings on 1st June 1961. The line into the sidings also crossed the London Transport line to Upminster on the level and in order not to disrupt their passenger services the changeovers usually took place at night.

On 23rd March 1961 I moved out of lodging accommodation in Tilbury into the Eastern region staff Hostel at Ilford, known as Aldersbrook House, which had been purpose-built in 1956 and, as there was a 24-hour meal service, it was ideal for railwaymen on shift work. Also in the hostel, besides footplate men, were a number of other LT&S staff including guards, shunters, signalmen, fitters and clerical staff. One of the shunting staff was John Jeremy who originated from East Anglia and who was employed at Grays. John's battered railway hat was well past its recycling date and even in the coldest of

The writer photographed in the cab of a Class 2–6–4T by his fireman, Maurice Edmunds, just prior to working an evening rush-hour train from Fenchurch Street to Southend. The left hand is seen resting on the reversing wheel and the right hand holding the regulator. Obscuring the right forearm is the cab equipment of the Hudd Automatic Warning System (AWS). This system was unique to the LT&S and preceded the later standard BR type. The top fitting housed the visual indicator whilst the handle to its left cancelled the apparatus when necessary.

weather he wore neither vest nor shirt, his chest being permanently exposed to the elements. When I was on the Grays' shunting engine with him I found him easygoing and a pleasure to work with. He had a good relationship with the female cooks in the hostel and when we were working together he would persuade them to give us bacon and eggs instead of the usual packed lunch; this enabled us to have a fry-up in his shunters cabin.

Generally very little has been written in railway literature concerning the role of the shunter, a man who was at the lower end of railwaymen's pay scale. Yet, a good shunter, who could work out the minimum number of moves to marshal a train, especially when the shunting yard was full of wagons, was worth his weight in gold. Of him it was said that he could use his head instead of his feet.

As the months went by, the electrification neared completion and, in order to be qualified to drive the new electric multiple units, drivers had to undergo a three-week retraining course. A full electric service was finally introduced on 18th June 1962 and what remained of the footplate staff eventually moved into a new purpose-built building, standing to one side of Tilbury Riverside station. To commemorate the closure of the steam shed, one of the drivers organised a farewell dinner dance. Amongst the invited guests was the well-liked Shed Master, Mr Clark, whom the drivers had nicknamed 'Tiger'. During

the course of the evening, the band was asked to play the popular tune 'Hold that Tiger' – he knew who it was aimed at! The electrification of the LT&S had been completed while continuing to run a heavy outer suburban passenger service with the minimum amount of disruption or delay, which was a great credit to all concerned. Needless to say, the media did not mention this fact; then, as now, the media gives maximum publicity to the railways' shortcomings but very little to their achievements.

With new signalling and the electric trains it was possible to run with a two-minute headway between trains. It was a strange sensation to be running at speed with the tail light of the preceding train clearly visible ahead. Higher speeds with the electrics were possible than with the heavy stock formations hauled by the 2–6–4 tanks. In the October 1962 edition of *Modern Railways*, Cecil J. Allen, in his 'Locomotive Running Past and Present' series of articles, published the log of a run by Mr H. T. Kirby in which he timed a train at 86½ m.p.h. at Dagenham East, considerably exceeding the permanent speed restriction of 75 m.p.h. Allen commented, 'I am not sure that speeds are to be commended on a line normally limited to 75 m.p.h. and with a train which has started punctually (the service was a midday one with 8 coaches), but I have included it as showing something of the potentialities of this new electric service'.

Two or three weeks after the publication of the magazine, drivers received a stern warning not to exceed permanent speed restrictions. Many drivers believed that this was as a direct result of Allen's article and, in this respect, they were probably right.

A few months after the introduction of the full electric service, it was realised that there was an over provision of staff at Tilbury and, as one of the junior drivers, I was, not for the first time, nor the last time in my railway career, declared redundant and consequently on 15th April 1963, I was moved to the LT&SR freight depot at Barking Ripple Lane. I was not altogether sorry, as after the initial novelty had worn off, driving the electrics had become somewhat tedious.

Acknowledgements:
Obstruction Danger by Adrian Vaughan – PSL 1989
London, Tilbury and Southend Railway and its Locomotives by R. J. Essery – OPC 2001
Fenchurch Street to Barking by J. F. Connor and Charles Phillips – Middleton Press 1998
Barking to Southend by Dr Edwin Course – Middleton press 2002
Tilbury Loop by Dr Edwin Course – Middleton Press 2002

Editor's Note
Although generally referred to as the LT&SR this company ceased to exist in 1912 when it became part of the Midland Railway. Post-1912 documents, etc, usually describe it as the LT&S Section.

LMS
TERRITORY

Lines that are not in the spotlight have always fascinated me and I offer this picture as an example of what I mean. This undated picture was taken at Bow Road and the note on the rear of the print states 'Freight from the LTS line passing Bow station'. Not being familiar with that part of the world, I assume that it is coming from Chalk Farm and I have included an extract from a Midland Railway Distance Diagram to show the lines around Bow, where, in addition to the North London Railway station, there were also two further Bow railway stations.

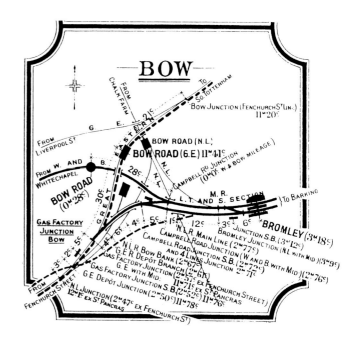

The picture shows one of the 0–6–0T engines, but the full number is not clear (752?). Introduced in 1889, some examples remained in service until the late 1950s, working on the Cromford and High Peak section. The number 49 was probably a Trip identification number, but note that the locomotive was not carrying headlamps, so it was not displaying a train classification code, which is rather unusual. I wonder if any knowledgeable readers can offer any additional information. In addition to the lack of a headlamp code, there are two other aspects that are worth considering. The first is the unusual position of the signal on the left of the picture, clearly placed at the back of the platform to give the best possible sighting to the enginemen. The second is the curious box on the platform ramp.
COLLECTION R. J. ESSERY

WARTIME AMBULANCES
A donation from two American railway companies
by NELSON TWELLS

THE outbreak of the Second World War on 3rd September 1939 marked the beginning of difficult times for Great Britain and its allies. Although America did not enter the war until December 1941, many Americans supported the war against Germany. An early indication of the comradeship and enthusiasm of American workers for the cause for which Britain was fighting was epitomised in 1941 by the generous presentation of three American motor ambulances to the LMS Railway Company.

The background to the presentation was that the LMS Railway Company had done much during the 1930s to foster good relationships with North American railroad companies by making two major gestures of support for the American railroad industry. The first was an agreement to transport the 'Royal Scot' locomotive,

No. 6100 *Royal Scot*, and the 1932 train of carriages to America for exhibition at the 'Century of Progress Exposition' that was held in Chicago in 1933. The second major LMS gesture was to ship the new 1938-built 'Coronation Scot' train and streamlined locomotive *Coronation* across the Atlantic, for exhibition at the 'New

York World's Fair' which opened mid-April 1939.

Both trains attracted great interest at the exhibitions and as they toured America, with the 'Royal Scot' train leaving the Chicago exhibition to travel west to Los Angeles, north to Vancouver and onto Canadian tracks, running east to Montreal,

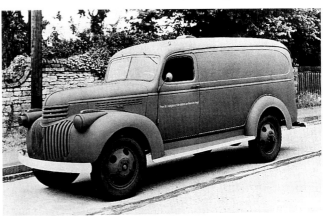

One of the three ambulances presented to the LMS, with lettering on the door 'From the Employees of the Central Railroad, New Jersey'.

Revised lettering: 'LMS Rly Ambulance' and Central Railroad reference.

One of the ambulances in use.

LMS Chairman Sir Thomas Royden helping Mrs. Somerville-Smith to alight from the rear of the ambulance.

before returning to Britain, whilst the 'Coronation Scot' tour was made in advance of the 1939 New York Fair. Much interest in the LMS and British railways in general, came from the huge numbers of people visiting the exhibitions, and also from the thousands who turned out to see the LMS trains during their respective tours across America. The enormous goodwill generated by the two tours was later reflected in the generous donation of the three ambulances to the LMS by railway staff on the Central Railroad, New Jersey, and the Reading Railroad, USA.

At a ceremony held at Euston on Thursday 24th July 1941, the three vehicles were formally presented to Sir Thomas Royden, Chairman of the LMS, by Mrs. Somerville-Smith, Representative in Britain of the British-American Ambulance Corps, who referred to the special mission on behalf of the American Ambulance Corps, by stressing 'the enthusiasm of American workers for the cause for which Britain is fighting'. Responding, the LMS Chairman referred to the 'touching gesture on the part of American railroad men in presenting these Ambulances to the LMS', and went on to say that '... no words could fittingly describe the depth of appreciation for the gifts which he regarded as a tribute to the way in which British railway workers generally had maintained essential services despite heavy air attacks by the enemy'. He also felt that 'they had been dedicated to the LMS in recognition of the Company's practical friendship towards the United States by sending its crack expresses, the 'Royal Scot' and later the 'Coronation Scot' on visits to the U.S.A. a few years ago.'

The three ambulances were to be allocated for use '... in densely populated areas served by the LMS – London, Birmingham, and Glasgow.' However, the reverse of the FNK 795 photograph states: 'They are being stationed at Glasgow, Derby and London'.

A further gesture around the same time, made towards Britain's war effort by the Baltimore & Ohio Railroad Company, was to 'the British Railways' of a Flying Ambulance for the Royal Air Force. It was stated at the presentation that initially, this had been intended for use in Britain, but, that '... it was more urgently needed in the Middle East where it had already been sent.'

[handwritten annotation:] EX MID. RLY 2183 CLASS BUILT SHARP STEWART 1892. H BOILERED c1907. REBUILT SUPERHEATED BELPAIRE TO "483" CONFIG. 1914 W[D]RN 1957. NOTTINGHAM 1920, 1927. AND 1935. DERBY 1944. AND 1956.

A Tour of Inspection over the Somerset & Dorset Line

by NEIL BURGESS

ONE of the fascinations of reading historical documents is the way they can open windows into the past in very direct ways, bringing other-wise long-forgotten events, sometimes very ordinary ones, into the present. Because the events they describe were then commonplace, it sometimes requires supplementary information to fill in the spaces left in the account because contem-poraries could take them for granted. This article attempts to do this with some mate-rial from Somerset & Dorset Joint Committee Minutes from 1931–47, cata-logued as RAIL 626/11 and in the care of the National Archives at Kew.

On Wednesday, 15th July 1936, the Somerset & Dorset Joint line between Bath and Broadstone Junction, including the branch from Evercreech Junction to Burnham-on-Sea, was inspected by four of the directors of the London, Midland and Scottish and the Southern railways, these being the Joint companies which owned and operated it. The line, original-ly created by the amalgamation of the Somerset Central and the Dorset Central railways in 1862, enjoyed a brief period of penurious independence until, almost bankrupted by its extension northwards to Bath, it fell into the hands of the Midland and the London & South Western rail-ways, much to the chagrin of the Great Western. The Somerset & Dorset Joint survived the 1923 Grouping as a joint undertaking, but in 1930 the LMS had assumed day-to-day control with the Southern responsible primarily for perma-nent way, signalling and civil engineering.[1] As recounted below, this was the start of a period of considerable upheaval on the line, undertaken against the background of the world Depression of the 'thirties and the changing fortunes of the railways as providers of inland transport in Britain. This article attempts not only to recon-struct the events of that day seventy years ago but also to try to understand the sig-nificance of the inspection in the context of the line's history.

Pursuing the conjecture in the article, the inspection train might have looked like this picture of Midland 2P 4–4–0 No. 418 hauling saloon No. 45016 along the main line near Churchdown in Gloucestershire. The date must be postwar since the line was quadrupled in 1942, with relief lines laid outside of the existing ones. AUTHOR'S COLLECTION

THE DIRECTORS

Each of the Joint companies was repre-sented by two directors.[2] For the LMS board were Sir Alan Garrett Anderson and Major Sir Ralph Glyn. Alan Anderson (1877–1952) was Chairman of Anderson Green & Co., who managed the Orient Line shipping company and was thereby the Chairman of the Orient board. He was a Deputy Lieutenant of the City of London and, between 1935 and 1940 its (Conservative) Member of Parliament. His mother was Elizabeth Garrett Anderson, the first woman to qualify and practise as a physician in Britain and also, after her retirement, the first woman to become a mayor. Sir Alan was Chairman of the Hospital Saving Association, one of the largest private medical insurance funds, with over two million subscribers, so he shared his mother's association both with politics and medicine. He had been one of the first chairmen of the International Chamber of Commerce (1926–1929) and in 1936 was appointed Chairman of a Board of Trade committee investigating the then new unit trusts. In 1941 he suc-

ceeded Sir Ralph Wedgwood of the LNER as Chairman of the Railway Executive and continued in that appoint-ment until the end of the war. He was concurrently Controller of Railways for the Ministry of War Transport.

Ralph Glyn (1885–1960) was a grand-son of the Duke of Argyll and had served with distinction as an officer during the Great War, seeing service at Gallipoli and in the Balkans. He was elected Conservative and Unionist MP for Clackmannan and East Stirlingshire in 1918, lost the seat in 1922 and was then elected to represent Abingdon in Berkshire in 1924. He was created a Baronet in 1934 and retained the seat in Abingdon until 1953 when he was created the first Baron Glyn.

The Southern was represented by Charles Forbes-Trelusis, twenty-first Baron Clinton, and Robert Holland-Martin. Lord Clinton (1863–1957) was an owner of considerable estates in Devon and lived at Heaton Sackville near Petrockstowe, appropriately served by a station on the LSWR line from Halwill

Junction to Barnstaple. He had been Chairman of the Forestry Commission between 1927 and 1932. In 2004 his successor to the title named a Wessex Trains class 150 diesel unit *The Lord Clinton*.

Robert Holland-Martin was Chairman of the Southern Railway board, having been elected in 1935 in succession to Lord Wakehurst, who had been Chairman since 1932. Holland-Martin remained in that office until 1944 when he was succeeded by Colonel Eric Gore-Brown and seems to have died soon afterwards.[3]

THE INSPECTION TRAIN

The report of the inspection, reproduced below, gives no details of the vehicles or motive power used on the day, but it is possible to speculate about them.[4] After the LMS took over day-to-day management of the Somerset & Dorset line in 1930 – the Southern were responsible for permanent way, signalling and civil engineering – the line was managed operationally under the Midland Division, based at Derby. This raises the possibility of two saloons[5] which might have been used. One was the Derby Operating Superintendent's vehicle, which in 1923 was Midland Railway No. 2234, a 1917 conversion of the company's sole steam railmotor. The conversion was at the behest of J. H. Follows, General Superintendent of the Midland, who used it extensively for tours of inspection all over the system, hauled until 1928 by Johnson bogie single No. 600. It is not clear whether 2234, renumbered 45010 by the LMS in 1933, was still based at Derby in 1936, but it is certainly a candidate for consideration if it was. Indeed, E. D. Grasett, the Divisional Superintendent of Operations at Derby, was in the party of LMS officials accompanying the directors, so it would presumably have been no difficulty for him to arrange for the saloon to be attached to a passenger train – most probably the down 'Pines Express' – the day before. Happily No. 45010 survived to be bought by George Dow and was presented to the National Railway Museum in 1978; it is currently (2007) at Locomotion, the NRM's collection at Shildon.

A second Midland saloon was No. 45016, built as a 32ft six-wheeled vehicle No. 124 in 1887 and rebuilt as a 54ft bogie vehicle, meanwhile renumbered 2552, in 1908. It survived to carry British Railway carmine and cream livery and was observed still in use at the rear of a down express at St. Pancras on 12th May 1959.[6]

The LMS possessed other inspection saloons, one of which was No. 45002, a most impressive 12-wheeler of LNWR origin. This would certainly have accommodated the party, but might have been out of gauge for the Somerset & Dorset: I am certainly unaware of any photographs of similarly-dimensioned vehicles in revenue-earning service over the line. The presence of directors could have caused No. 45000, the LMS Chairman's saloon, to be used, but it had a limited seating capacity and would have required another vehicle to accompany it. No. 45000 was very prestigious, being included in the royal train on occasions, and was possibly too much so to be considered for this duty. The Midland vehicles might therefore be the most likely, though, as noted earlier, this is speculative.

There is a possibility that another saloon might have been used; this was the Southern Railway's No. 1s, a 46ft bogie vehicle built in 1885 for the directors of the London & South Western Railway. This would certainly have been the most

Saloon M45016M on the rear of a down express at St. Pancras on 12th May 1959.   MARTIN S. WELCH

likely specialised vehicle to be used had it fallen to the Southern to provide the inspection train.[7]

It is equally difficult to be certain about the motive power used on the day, but the Midland '483' class 4–4–0s, and their LMS successors, the '563' class, were often to be seen on these duties and thirteen of them were allocated to the Somerset & Dorset in 1936, the only specifically passenger types on the line.[8]

WHY MAKE THE INSPECTION?

This is the only Directors' inspection recorded in the Joint Committee minutes between 1918 and 1947 and it is interesting to speculate why it was arranged when it was. The LMS had assumed effective day-to-day control of the line in 1930 and it might have been thought that this could have been a suitable occasion for a tour of inspection; but nothing seems to have been arranged. Whilst is possible that the 1936 inspection was simply something that had been intended for some time but never undertaken until then, it may be that there was rather more calculation about the date than this.

As I have discussed elsewhere[9], in 1930 the LMS management entertained no illusions about the Somerset & Dorset line as a commercial asset and they clearly saw it primarily as a through route allowing the company access to the south coast independently of the Great Western, rather than as much of a generator of income in its own right. No sooner had the changes in management been effected than the LMS began a campaign of seeking operating economies which lasted throughout the 1930s and would have continued to bite ever deeper had not war intervened in 1939. In addition to very obvious measures such as the closure of Highbridge works, the LMS sought reductions in staffing, motive power and train services which must have been deeply unpopular as Britain sank into the trough of the Depression of the early 1930s.

However, in order to fulfil its role as a through route, it was also clear that alongside the economies there would need to be a programme of investment in the line. The minutes of the Joint Committee's officers indicate that from the late 1920s there was a growing awareness that arrears in maintenance had been allowed to build up under the old management, particularly over the state of the track; and that there had been no modernisation of facilities to keep pace with the economic realities of the early Grouping period. Many of these matters required urgent attention and it is entirely probable that some of the economies in other areas were made the more necessary in order to allow investment in the Joint line. Many of these investments had been made, or were about to be made, by 1936. The Joint Committee officers' minutes record 68 instances of improvements being agreed between 1930 and 1947, of which 24 were agreed by 1936 and a further 22 by the outbreak of war in 1939. It is clear from the report of the inspection that one of its purposes was to allow some of these works to be viewed by the directors, but it was probable that the date was chosen because it allowed the management to show that the line was now in significantly better order than in 1930. 1936 is also significant since there had been the creation of facilities for new categories of traffic, not least bulk milk in tankers; connections to dairies at Bason Bridge on the Highbridge line and Wincanton and Bailey Gate on the section south of Evercreech Junction were included on the directors' itinerary. The lifting of the economic hardships of the Depression were becoming apparent in many areas of Britain by the mid-thirties and holiday and excursion traffic was growing modestly. The Southern was also making investments which affected the Somerset & Dorset, not least the rebuilding of Templecombe station on the Salisbury–Exeter line, which had been agreed at the time of the inspection and actually undertaken in 1938. For all these reasons the management may have felt they had something to show to the directors which marked both progress to date and anticipations of future improvements.

THE INSPECTION

The details of the inspection were recorded in the minutes as follows:

Directors' Visit of Inspection; Wednesday 15th July 1936

Present
Southern Railway Company
R. Holland-Martin, Esq., CB.
The Right Hon. Lord Clinton, PC., GCVO.

attended by:
W. Bishop, Esq. (Solicitor)
G. Ellson, Esq. (Chief Engineer)
R. G. Davison, Esq. (Joint Accountant)
Major L. F. S. Dawes (Secretary)
W. H. Shortt, Esq. (Divisional Engineer)

Present
London Midland & Scottish Railway Company
Sir Alan G. Anderson, GBE., MP.
Major Sir Ralph Glyn, Bart. MC., DL., MP.

attended by:
H. V. Mosley, Esq. (CEO for New Works, etc)
E. Taylor, Esq. (Chief Accountant)
S. B. Carter, Esq. (Outdoor Superintendent)
W. H. C. Clay, Esq. (Estate Agent)
D. C. McCulloch, Esq. (Commercial Manager's Assistant)
E. D. Grasett, Esq. (Divisional Supt. of Operations Derby)
D. S. Macdonald, Esq. (Secretary of Joint Conference)
S. Sealy, Esq. (District Controller, Bath)

The party left Bath station by special train at 9.30 am. passing through Combe Down Tunnel and Midford.

A stop was made at RADSTOCK where the scheme for modification of the layout of the yard with a view to reduction in cost of renewal and maintenance, referred to in Joint Committee Minutes nos. 4932 and 4950, is being carried out.

There are direct connections from the railway to the Middle Pit, Ludlows, and Tynings Collieries.

Passing MIDSOMER NORTON it was noted that trouble, considered to be attributable to the workings at Norton Hill Colliery, had been experienced by reason of the movement of the embankment and retaining wall adjoining the main road which passes under the line at the Radstock end of the station. Careful records of the existing contour and inclination of the retaining wall have been taken and the matter is being watched. The Colliery Company does not at present admit liability.

SHEPTON MALLET (stop). Special cattle van washing facilities have recently been provided at a cost of £105 in connection with a large bacon factory constructed on land belonging to the Joint Committee by the Co-operative Wholesale Society.

At EVERCREECH JUNCTION the station and works generally were inspected, after which the train proceeded up the single track branch line to Burnham, Wells and Bridgwater.

A stop was made at GLASTONBURY where the scheme for re-arrangement of the sidings and roadways in the Goods Yard, sanctioned by Joint Committee Minute no.4960, with a view to effect a saving in the cost of renewal and maintenance, will be put into operation as and when reconditioning in the ordinary course becomes necessary.

The offices forming part of the disused Engineering Department accommodation which have been converted into two bungalows under the authority of Joint Committee Minute no.4862, and the house and gardens known as 'The Pollards' were inspected.

Bridges nos. 286 and 287 which were recently reconstructed in ferro-concrete under the authority of Joint Committee Minute no. 4876 (6th Feb.1935) were noted in passing.

At WELLS a short stop was made and the station and general layout of the tracks were examined.

Passing ASHCOTT the reconstruction of the platform in reinforced concrete to reduce dimensions (referred to in Joint Committee Minute no. 4875 6th Feb.1935) was noted.

At BASON BRIDGE (stop), where the Wilts United Dairies have a large factory, additional siding accommodation has been provided under the author-

A fortuitous moment at Cole during 1938, with a northbound passenger train in the charge of an ex-Midland 2P passing a down goods, behind a 7F 2–8–0. The goods comprised mainly open wagons, some of those at the front being sheeted and some possibly for the conveyance of either china clay from Wadebridge or ball clay from Purbeck; but most were minerals. Though hidden by the parapet of the bridge carrying the line over the Great Western's Berks & Hants extension to Taunton, it is just possible to discern one of the six-wheeled road brake vans built for the Somerset & Dorset from the late 1880s. The passenger train was another LSWR 3-set, this time probably non-corridor stock (BTL+CL+BTL) which also saw extensive use over the line after 1930. LMS coaches top and tail the 3-set, a period 1 corridor third behind the engine and an LNWR arc-roof full brake at the rear.

AUTHOR'S COLLECTION

A down goods rolling through Shepton Mallet, where the inspection party alighted in 1936, headed by large-boilered 7F 2-8-0 No. 53807. Again, the preponderance of open wagons, mainly minerals, typifies many such workings over the Somerset & Dorset down to closure. The date is some time between April 1950, when 53807 received its BR number, and June 1954 when it was rebuilt with the smaller G9AS boiler.
J. H. MOSS

ity of Joint Committee Minute no. 4790 (3rd May 1933) for dealing with the increasing milk traffic of the firm. The gross value of such traffic has increased from £22,900 in 1931 to £45,142 in 1935

At HIGHBRIDGE inspection was made of:-

a). The two-span reinforced concrete footbridge with three stairways recently constructed in conjunction with the Great Western Railway Company in replacement of the old semi-independent footbridges (see Joint Committee Minute no. 4851 18th July 1934);

b). The layout of the sidings in the marshalling yard which is being undertaken in the next few years (see Joint Committee Minute no. 4850 same date);

c). The Committee's Wharf, the practice with regard to the clearance of mud therefrom being explained;

d). The disused Carriage and Wagon Erecting Shop which has been leased to Mr. Ashford for use as a piggery (see Joint Committee Minute no. 4840 2nd May 1934).

BURNHAM-on-SEA. The station was inspected, it having been previously explained that the passenger traffic, largely consisting of short journeys from Highbridge, would not justify any considerable improvement on station improvement.

After returning over the Burnham Branch to Evercreech Junction a stop was made at WINCANTON where Messrs. Cow & Gate, Ltd., recently erected a large factory adjoining the Committee's property, with direct siding access from the Committee's yard, the cost of which was borne by the firm (see Joint Committee Minute no. 4815 8th Nov. 1933).

At TEMPLECOMBE Upper Station the station improvements recently authorised by the Southern Railway Company, which will effect considerable improvement in the platform used by the Somerset & Dorset trains and the accommodation available for passengers by them were considered and noted.

Lord Clinton left the party at Templecombe, and the special train then returned to the Joint Line and proceeded to BAILEY GATE where the siding accommodation provided for the United Dairies, Ltd., under the authority of Joint Committee Minute no.4726 (3rd Feb. 1932) and the Dairy Company's Cheese Works were visited.

The inspection concluded at Bournemouth.

WORKING THE TRAIN

The report indicates stops *en route* at Radstock, Shepton Mallet and Evercreech Junction; then onto the Highbridge line to Glastonbury, reversing up the branch to Wells, then calling at Bason Bridge, a lengthy stop at Highbridge covering the works, station and wharf before proceeding to Burnham; then back along 'the Branch' to Evercreech, with stops at Wincanton, Templecombe and Bailey Gate before running on to Bournemouth. To do this the special would have to keep out of the way of regular service trains, which can be summarised as:[10]

10.22 Passenger, Bath–Bournemouth West, stopping at most stations
11.30 Through Goods, Bath–Evercreech Junction
1/00 Passenger, Wells–Glastonbury
1/15 Passenger, Glastonbury–Wells
1/10 Passenger, Bath–Templecombe, stopping at all stations
2/20 Express Passenger, Bath–Bournemouth West, calling at principal stations (the 'Pines Express')
3/45 Passenger, Bournemouth West–Bath and Bristol (the 'Up Mail')
4/00 Express Passenger, Bath–Bournemouth West, calling at principal stations

Such goods trains as were running during the day would probably not have affected the special. Its departure from Bath at 9.30 meant that it would have followed the 9.20 Bath–Bournemouth passenger train which called at Evercreech Junction and Poole only. If the special made the same time as the 9.20 it would have reached Radstock by 9.49. As long as it left before 10.43 it would have kept ahead of the 10.22. Based on the timings of the 9.20, it could then have reached Shepton Mallet by 11.07, seven minutes ahead of the 10.22. It might have been shunted aside to allow the service train to pass, in which case it could take its time to Evercreech Junction as long as it kept ahead of the 11.30 Bath–Evercreech goods, due to take water at Shepton at 1/06. Since Evercreech was eleven minutes' running from Shepton Mallet, an arrival somewhere around mid-day would have kept the special out of the way of traffic on 'the Branch' as long as it left Evercreech before the departure of the 12/40 to Burnham. It might have been possible either to get to Wells before the 1/00 train came down to Glastonbury, or else might have followed its return journey at 1/15. After leaving Wells, it would have been a matter of keeping ahead of the 3/45 from Evercreech on the journey down to Highbridge and it is entirely possible that the special would have arrived there before the 3/00 from Burnham left at 3/05. Running back to Evercreech, the 'Pines Express' should have been long gone – departing at 3/12 – allowing the special a clear path to Templecombe. The 4/00 Bath – Bournemouth express would be due to pass Templecombe at 5/17, so either running ahead to Bailey Gate and being shunted, or else following behind, the special could have made Bournemouth by around 7/00 at the latest. Because the section between Templecombe and Blandford was single track, it would also have been necessary to avoid the 3/45 up passenger from Bournemouth to Bristol, due out of Blandford at 4/32 – the more so because this was the 'Up Mail', which needed to connect with the 7/20 Bristol to York postal express at Mangotsfield. Allowing that leaving and rejoining the train to inspect locations might have taken longer than anticipated, and that it may have been more or less difficult to shepherd the directors around, there was still a good deal of leeway with the timetable.

Two other operational matters might be mentioned. The first is that the special would have required no guard, since his operational duties on the day could be carried out by one of the inspection party; no doubt the wage grade staff would take a keen interest to see whether 'the bosses' managed to carry them out satisfactorily. The saloon would, however, have carried an attendant whose duties would have included keeping the party supplied with refreshments and possibly some kind of meal. Many inspections seem to have included a stop at which the party would have decamped to some suitable place for a sit-down meal, but there is no mention of such a stop in the report. It might have

been at Highbridge, or even Burnham, where advantage might have been taken of one of the hotels on the sea front.

The other point is that inspection saloons could be either hauled engine-first or propelled, thus removing the necessity for running-round at terminals and also offering the opportunity for unrivalled views of the line through the saloon's end windows: Midland saloon no. 45016 also had an open balcony at one end, on which the party might have congregated, weather permitting, for the same purpose. Indeed running round might have posed other problems since a system of electric bells was often rigged up to allow some rudimentary communication between the saloon and the enginemen, should it be required to stop the saloon in the section. It is reasonable to suppose that at least as the train traversed the branches to Burnham and Wells, this method of operation was employed.

It is now seventy years since this inspection was undertaken and forty since the Somerset & Dorset line succumbed to the Beeching Report and was finally closed as a through route. Today the line is generally remembered by enthusiasts for the procession of summer Saturday workings to and from the south coast during the 1950s and early 1960s; but the railway the directors and management inspected on that July day in 1936 had not yet begun to take on that role – though excursions were common enough even then – and their interests were more in the financial and operational realities of the system. There is no mention in the minutes of whether the

inspection was deemed to have been successful, but it is good to think that, as they made their ways home afterwards, the managers at least thought it had been.

Notes

1. This is the general position, though the Southern continued to supply some of the coaching stock used on the line throughout the period up to nationalisation in 1948.
2. Biographical details of the directors are taken from several editions of *Who Was Who*: Holland-Martin is not listed there so reference was made to C. F. Dendy-Marshall's *History of the Southern Railway Vol. 2*, as revised by R. W. Kidner (Ian Allan: 1963).
3. The Southern's official history of the railway in wartime, Bernard Darwin's *War on the Line* (1946: reprinted by Middleton Press 1984 and 1993) refers to him as 'the late Mr. Robert Holland Martin' (p. 195).
4. I am indebted to my fellow LMS Society member Martin Welch, a BR civil engineer, for much of the information in this section.
5. Details of both Midland vehicles are in R. E. Lacy & George Dow: *Midland Railway Carriages Vol. 2*: Wild Swan Publications (1986), chapter 12.
6. This information is from Martin Welch (above): Lacy & Dow indicate that, 'it is believed to have survived until November 1956'; in any event, it was long-lived.
7. Details of No. 1s are given in G. R. Weddell's *LSWR Carriages, Vol. 1 1838–1900*: Wild Swan Publications (1992), chapter 5.
8. There were, of course, other types, such as the Johnson 3F and Fowler 4F 0–6–0s which were used on passenger trains, even though officially designated goods engines. 4Fs, or 'Armstrongs', were even to be seen on the 'Pines Express'.
9. See 'Making Economies on the Somerset & Dorset, 1929–31': in *LMS Journal*: No. 6, 2004, pp. 31–39.
10. Information from the Working timetable for 6th July–27th September 1936.

[handwritten annotation] LMS STANDARD 2P BUILT TO OLD MID. RLY '483' CONFIG. DERBY 1930 (6'9" DRIVERS INSTEAD OF 7'0") WIDRAWN 1961.

A 1937 scene on the Somerset & Dorset line south of Templecombe which typifies several aspects of its operation following the LMS assuming day-to-day control in 1930. The engine, LMS 2P No. 629, was one of a number transferred to Bath to replace the miscellaneous collection of 4-4-0 tender engines inherited from the Joint Committee. The passenger accommodation was provided by an LSWR corridor 3-set (BTK+CK+BCK) which were drafted onto the line by the Southern as successors to the various S&D non-corridor coaches it obtained when the Joint Committee's coaching stock was divided between the owning companies. The passenger full brake behind this is unidentified – possibly of LNWR origin judging by the toplights in the sides. The two six-wheeled milk tanks were signs of the new traffic which the railways were trying to capture during the decade.

H. C. CASSERLEY